SUZUKI
TWO-STROKES

OSPREY
COLLECTOR'S
LIBRARY

SUZUKI TWO-STROKES

All two-stroke singles,
twins and triples
(plus RE5)—1952 to 1979

Roy Bacon

Published in 1984 by Osprey Publishing Limited
12–14 Long Acre, London WC2E 9LP
Member company of the George Philip Group

© Copyright Roy Bacon 1984

This book is copyrighted under the Berne Convention. All rights reserved. Apart from any fair dealing for the purpose of private study, research, criticism or review, as permitted under the Copyright Act, 1956, no part of this publication may be reproduced, stored in a retrieval system, or transmitted in any form or by any means, electronic, electrical, chemical, mechanical, optical, photocopying, recording, or otherwise, without prior written permission. All enquiries should be addressed to the publisher.

British Library Cataloguing in Publication Data

Bacon, Roy H.
   Suzuki two-strokes
   1. Suzuki motorcycles—History
   I. Title
   629.2'275   TL448.S8
ISBN 0-85045-588-X

Editor Tim Parker
Filmset and Printed in England by
BAS Printers Limited, Over Wallop, Hampshire

Contents

    Foreword by Roger de Coster   7
    Acknowledgements   8
1   Ancestors in Hamamatsu   10
2   Road singles   27
3   Off-road singles   50
4   Little twins, big twins   71
5   Air or liquid triples   102
6   Rotary motion   126
7   Motocross   139
8   Road racing   149

Appendix
1   Specifications   163
2   Names, numbers and letters   183
3   Model recognition   184
4   Carburettor settings   187
5   Model chart   190

Foreword by Roger de Coster

I am happy to write a foreword to this book on the history of the Suzuki two-strokes by Roy Bacon, for Suzuki wrote the foreword to my career and probably for the rest of my life.

When I started racing 20 years ago, I didn't consider much beyond training during the week and racing motocross on Sundays. Business and commercial interests didn't enter into my world. So, when I went one Sunday in 1965, to race in the Belgian 250 cc Grand Prix at Mont Kemmel near the Belgian/French border, I had little idea that on that day, I would come face to face with my future and witness the first thrust of the Japanese two-wheeled invasion. Mont Kemmel is a large hill with a hotel on top and a motocross circuit winding around it that overlooks flat fields and hedgerows where 50 years before, thousands of soldiers had lost their lives in trenches trying to capture the hill we were racing on. On this day in terrible, muddy conditions, there appeared a small team of Japanese riders. Torsten Hallman won the race from my old friend Joel Robert and myself. The two Japanese riders, Kubo and Kojima, didn't finish but they left their mark. Suzuki had arrived in motocross . . . and into my life. Everyone looked at and studied the new machinery. The Japanese in turn studied and took pictures of every bike in the paddock and departed.

Five years later I was to join the Suzuki team, winning their first 500 cc Motocross World Championship in 1971 and repeating it for them in 1972, 1973, 1975 and 1976. It was success built around sound engineering and a desire by the people at Suzuki to win. My first contract came with a letter stating bluntly, 'we confirm contract and terms. We are glad and ready to win all World Championships.'! I have had a long and happy relationship with Suzuki, the Japanese and the people at Hamamatsu.

I am happy to preface this book for Suzuki has not only had a major impact on myself, motocross, road racing, street riding and trail riding, but Suzuki has, and will in the future have, a big impact in the world of transport. From nothing in the 1920s, Suzuki two, three- and four-wheelers now haul logs in forests, work on farms in the Third World and move people worldwide. Having read this book, it gives me an insight I didn't have before, for Suzuki and motocross are two subjects that always intrigued me most. In years to come Suzuki will be a part of transportation history, with the sporting side just part of spreading the word, in which maybe I helped by winning World Championships for them. This book will be a reference for the future, about the past.

I thank Suzuki for myself and will always have great memories of the people at Hamamatsu, in particular Mr E. Yokouchi and Mr H. Tamaki. I thank Roy Bacon for writing this book . . . it educated me and I hope it sets out the record for others. If you have been brushed by Suzuki, the sport and motorcycling, then you should make your knowledge complete. I'm glad I did.

Roger de Coster
World 500 cc Motocross Champion riding Suzuki
1971–73, 1975, 1976
California, USA
July 1984

The superb style of a five times world champion. Roger de Coster at the French GP in 1975

Acknowledgements

Riding press model Suzukis in the seventies usually gave rise to the thought that all their testers must have long arms as the bars often seemed an inch or so too far forward. There was seldom much else to complain of which maybe has a bearing on the one now in my garage.

One of the first memories of the Suzuki two-stroke came in practice for the 1962 TT. As I went into Union Mills on my small 125, this diminutive works 50 swept under my handlebars and drove away up the hill, changing many gears. No wonder they lapped at 75 mph in the race.

Writing this history for Osprey was aided by many friends but especially by Simon Parker of Heron Suzuki GB. He provided me with data, specifications and brochures which enabled me to write the book and he then checked it to see where I had gone wrong and to correct the mistakes. Others from the Crawley works who helped were Ian Catford and Peter Agg, the chairman of Heron Suzuki who gave the project his blessing.

Ex-Heron Suzuki, now Lancar or Lancia, friend and fellow scribe Ray Battersby, guided me to sources of data. From outside the company Bran Bardsley offered help from his long standing knowledge of Suzukis old and new while for the RE5 I turned to Geoff Monty who is the UK specialist for that model.

The Le Mans America club played its part in my search and president Ed Quinn put me in touch with historian Ken Storms who lent material which proved most useful.

The pictures came from many sources and again I have to thank our two major suppliers first – they are Jim Lindsay of *Mechanics* and Ron Beacham i/c the EMAP archives who now hold the old *Motor Cycle Weekly* files. Many pictures were from Heron Suzuki GB and some from the parent company in Japan. The National Motor Museum at Beaulieu was as always a helpful source and from their private files both Simon Parker of Suzuki and long time friend Mole Benn lent me material.

Quite a number of the pictures were taken by the professionals and in their number were Ashley-Color, Malcolm Carling, DPPI, Francis Goodman, Jan Hesse, Brian Holder, Institute of Motorcyling, Douglas Jackson, Bruce Main-Smith, John Neal, I. Nilsson, Toshi Nishiyma, Frank O'Shanohun Associates, Donald Page, Tim Parker, Penfold Studios, Maurice Spalding and P. Worden.

As usual the pictures were returned to their source and I have tried to make contact to clear copyright. If my letter failed to reach you or I have used an unmarked print without knowing this, I can only apologize.

To end these acknowledgements I must thank the evergreen Roger de Coster for kindly writing the foreword and Tim Parker with fellow author/photographer Gerald Foster for finding him. He's still riding off-road but most of it in America. As ever the Osprey editorial staff have my gratitude for their help and forbearance. May it long continue. . . .

Roy Bacon
Niton, Isle of Wight
June 1984

1 Ancestors in Hamamatsu

Michio Suzuki was a successful loom maker long before he built his first motorcycle and near retirement when the company that now carries his name first went into the production of them. Even then it was to be some time before the now familiar stylized S was seen for at first the brand name Colleda was used and the initials SJK.

Suzuki himself was born in 1887 in the small village that was than Hamamatsu and is now the city in which the company is based. In his early teens he served a seven year apprenticeship as a carpenter and a year after its end, when 22, launched his own business. His father was a cotton farmer and in his youth he had helped in the fields so he knew the raw material. His apprentice master had been involved in loom making so he utilized both areas of his knowledge and training to go into their manufacture.

As with most such enterprises the early days were hard but his father helped by giving him an old silk worm raising hut. In this the young Michio gathered scrap wood and iron and quickly designed, made and assembled his first treadle loom. He gave it to his mother who found it a great improvement on her existing one, the word spread and Suzuki was busy in his business.

From 1909 onwards the firm expanded and prospered, exporting its wares into South East Asia and India. It rode out various ups-and-downs of the Japanese economy over the next three decades and the technical excellence of the product plus various inventions from Michio

The Diamond Free engine unit with 2-speed gearbox in bicycle with twin top tube and rear mounted fuel tank. Note split exhaust

along the way kept the firm very solvent.

While the success of the looms was very pleasing Suzuki looked ahead and in the mid 1930s considered the time ripe for some diversification. He decided to try the transport field and in 1937 built a prototype motorcycle engine and a complete car based on an Austin 7. This followed the lines of the English vehicle with a 4-cylinder, side valve engine of 750 cc coupled to a 4-speed gearbox. The car was an open tourer and aluminium was used for a number of the major castings.

This enterprise did not come to anything for the military government of the day informed Suzuki that it was a frivolous non-essential and suggested he made munitions. He did—until 1945.

If diversification had seemed a potentially good idea in 1937 it was an essential in 1946. The factories were damaged, large sums were owed to the firm but cash was short and there was a hefty payroll to meet. Looms were certainly needed but were expensive items that took time to build and longer to get paid for. Materials were short and the need was to make something, anything, that could be sold for cash at once.

So Suzuki had his men making anything and everything to keep the company going and the cash rolling in. Farm implements were one line and a good one for the farmers needed tools, springs for raising windows were another while equally diverse was a venture into drum covers.

Complete Diamond Free transport in 1953 with crash bars and telescopic forks, one of many variations

Tools such as pliers were made and electric heaters to combat the cold weather.

Even the loom business picked up in time and it looked as if the company was riding out the economic storms of the unstable conditions of the late 1940s. Then in 1949 came a major crisis. At that time the country was still occupied and under the MacArthur administration which continued until it became independant in 1952. In 1949 it was on the brink of revolution and to many the Suzuki company represented the worst aspects of industry and the militarists of the 1930s.

The result was controversy over future company plans and then a hard 6 month strike which crippled production and indirectly set the firm onto the path of two wheels. Michio Suzuki was now 63 and sought peace and quiet from his factory problems by going fishing. To get well away from the street crowds he used a bicycle as did most in Japan in those days for there were few cars and limited public transport.

For a man in his sixties and a company head it was undignified to have to scrabble for a seat on a tram, and not easy with fishing tackle. The bicycle overcame that problem but was rather slow and rather hard work, more so with age and when beset with industrial troubles.

Whatever started the train of thought is not known but Michio could see very clearly that a small engine would make it so much easier to reach the fishing spot. He could also see that others had already put that thought into material form to meet the vast, virtually untapped market for cheap personal transport. He did not think too highly of some of the contraptions that passed him on the road or that he passed when their owners were forced to carry out some essential task of maintenance. And perhaps there was a

An early 4-stroke, the 1955 COX of 90 cc, ohv, channel steel frame and plunger rear

touch of pride too to push him along, pride in the many improvements he had brought into the loom industry. If he could do it with one product, then why not with another and so build a better motorcycle than the next man. So Michio began to look at the machines round him and to learn their origins and history.

The background of many was similar and very short. A small firm, a supply of war surplus engines or units from another firm, bought-in components and another name joined the lists and another smoking, inefficient and rattling model was on the road.

The history went back rather further and even in Japan as far back as 1908 when their first machine was built by Torao Yamaba. He built an engine and bolted it to a bicycle but a year later one N. Shimazu built a complete machine with 400 cc engine and direct belt drive. This was not to be the fore-runner of massive production for in the years ahead few Japanese machines were built. Up to the first war the numbers were miniscule for the bikes were crude and roads few in a country that still travelled by boat when it travelled at all.

After the Great War a middle class with modern ideas appeared in Japan and they accepted the notion of personal transport on two wheels. A law of the times assisted this for cars were restricted in width so they could traverse the bridges and negotiate the narrow streets. A motorcycle was easier to manage in these conditions but it was foreign ones that sold with models from England, Germany, Belgium and the USA flooding onto the market.

The infant Japanese industry nearly died there and then. It tried to match Western knowledge in a few areas and in 1921 the first overhead valve engine was built, a year before the great Norton firm moved their valve upstairs. Sadly the Japanese engine lacked power and was not destined to go on to TT victories and a long line of road models as its English contemporary did. In 1923 Musashino Kogyo built an engine using all home manufactured parts which was an incredible claim for the time. Then, it was normal practice for items such as magneto, carburettor and gears to be imported with just the bare essentials cast in Japan.

The Japanese industry was rescued by the government passing a bill which allowed it to offer subsidies to makers of vehicles suitable for military use as long as they were made in Japan. This galvanized them into action and while some results were totally unacceptable to the army others did become popular and were made in reasonable quantities.

The snag was that what they built was not reliable, not very powerful and totally without spares. The very concept of making parts to a drawing was only applied to a complete unit. You built an engine and if the valves failed you began again or made something to suit. The whole world of engineering tolerances and fits was unknown.

So the Harley Davidson vee-twins continued to dominate the market and made up most of the imports with only one in five machines coming from their oriental homeland. During the 1920s this worsened Japan's balance of payments problems and by the end of the decade they had established a ministry sponsored committee to curb imports. In counter to this was a desperate need for the army to equip itself with motorized transport and at that period the military men dominated the government. In 1935 they passed a further law that precluded foreign companies and money while over the next year or so raised the tariffs of imported motorcycles to a very high level.

Meanwhile Harley-Davidson had suffered from the depression and were quite happy to make some quick cash by selling the rights of an old and obsolete model to Japan. What was far more important than the drawings of the machine was the background know-how they also passed over. The mysteries of heat treatment of steels was just one aspect that came across. In addition senior Harley men went to Japan and showed how to set up a modern factory. They taught workshop cleanliness, precision manufacture to drawings, inspection, quality control, assembly line techniques and all the many facets that enable man to build complex machines in large numbers.

The resultant motorcycle was the Rikuo and the factory it was built in was soon the high spot of a tour for the top industry men of Japan who took home the lessons given and applied them to their own business. Perhaps Michio Suzuki was among them or maybe he just delegated the trip to a junior. Unlikely for his inventive mind would have delighted in the new technology and the challenge of adapting it to his loom business.

The Japanese motorcycle industry was still a small affair and much of the production was of the Rikuo model with some 18,000 being produced up to 1945. To put their industry into perspective their best year up to then was 1940 with just over 3000 machines built while in the year earlier England produced twenty times that number and Germany more than three times the English quantity. Real Japanese production, discounting the Harley copies, was very small *sakana* indeed.

After 1945 it all changed. The occupation brought an end to the economic cartels, the *zaibatsu*, that had controlled so much in the thirties. Then, no mechanic by the name of Honda with a few tools could explode into business but postwar he could. Transport was a basic need in desperately short supply so many small firms set out to meet it. They bought up Tohatsu and Mikuni surplus army engines and bolted them to bicycles. When the surplus ran out they besieged any firm that could make an engine and paid cash on the nail. They carried sacks of yen to make sure they could buy anything and everything that resembled a motorcycle engine.

This era began to change for something with more stability before Suzuki dipped a corporate toe in the water. The worst of the backyard designs disappeared and the whole industry changed up a gear. There were still many firms on the scene but they were now manufacturers in much more real terms than before and producing in some quantity. The competition was still tough and became tougher.

From 1952 official government policy was to buy Japanese. Around the same time tariff walls in the form of import duties and special taxes above them were erected. Firms who used motorcycles and received government contracts found themselves under pressure to buy Japanese machines if they wanted to see any more contracts. Then in 1955 it was made impossible for a private citizen to buy a foreign bike. At that point the banks could and would refuse to change your yen into English pounds, German marks or US dollars so there was no way you could raise a bank draft. Export of yen was banned, so the average Japanese either bought home produce or walked.

The exception to the tariff rules was any company in the business who wanted to buy a foreign sample to study. For them the tariffs went, along with import dues and other taxes, as the government encouraged such keenness to learn. They would even lend the money to buy the machine and the Japanese engineers studied their lessons with care.

Behind the tariff wall a war went on throughout the fifties. It was fought for the motorcycle market and to the eastern code, without mercy or prisoners. Over 100 combatants entered the arena and like the Samurai of old they battled according to their own rules, ethics and standards. In a few short years only eight remained and in time they shrunk to the big four who had stayed the course.

Early in their struggle firms had copied the best

The Mini-Free 50 cc moped with belt drive, strutted bicycle fork and drum rear brake

The first ST model, a 123 cc 2-stroke with three speeds and plunger frame. Sold as SJK make

and worst from Europe, and the survivors were those who copied the very best from Germany and Italy and who then moved on. By the end of the decade the fierce competition had weeded out the weak to leave the strong with new factories equipped with the very latest machine tools.

With them they built bikes in vast numbers powered by engines that were now better than anything they had first inspected. Their copying days were now well behind them and the massive home market mopped up a million machines a year. This was a production rate quite outside the ken of European firms and it was all taken by the Japanese themselves or their local export market in South East Asia. Half a world away no-

one had heard of Meguro, Tohatsu, Monarch, Ito, Hosk, Cabton or the many others that had fallen.

A 1956 feature in *The Motor Cycle* acknowledged that Eastern machines came closer each year to those built in the West and pictured Olympus, Showa, Lilac, Martui, Liner, DNB and Asabi among others. They show marked English, German or Italian lines of that time and from that base the Japanese engineers learnt very quickly. As firms went under the men moved elsewhere always learning new techniques, new skills, new designs and in a few short years had accumulated in-depth knowledge of most European styles and trends.

They put this to use and by the end of the decade, with the home market saturated, began to look overseas. In Japan they would now only sell replacements so, to keep their business going and expanding, needed new sales territories worldwide.

It was an odd situation for by then Japan was the foremost producer of motorcycles in the world and most of the world had never heard of them. It was a far cry from the 3000 machines built in 1940.

Suzuki were well involved by the end of the fifties for the result of Michio's thoughts and studies in 1951 was a decision to make a small engine to attach to a bicycle. He refused to consider the use of war surplus motors and really that era had ended by then anyway.

Something a little better was what was needed and he decided the way to do this was to make the entire unit himself including magneto, carburettor and oil seals. He also decided that the best place to mount the engine was in the middle of the machine just above the pedals and to drive the rear wheel by chain. This was in marked contrast to most other makes which used proprietary parts, hung the engines on anywhere and drove a tyre with a friction roller.

The Suzuki engine was a 2-stroke of 36 cc with a vertical cylinder, carburettor at the rear, exhaust in front running down under the frame, and magneto on the right. A countershaft chain drove a sprocket mounted outboard of the normal pedalling one and the whole engine and its chain drive was enclosed with panels. They carried its name which was Byc. Power Free.

There were development problems at first, for Suzuki were designing in a completely new field quite outside their experience and running into the difficulties of engine production for the first time. Initially the oil seals, handcut in leather, leaked, the flywheel refused to stay keyed to the crankshaft and the carburettor float sunk.

In time all these troubles were overcome and the units went on sale. The most popular feature proved not to lie in the engine at all but in its transmission. The sprockets were designed so that the rider could assist the engine by pedalling, let the engine do all the work or, if it failed, pedal the bicycle without turning the engine over.

A few months later the engine was enlarged to 50 cc and a 2-speed gear introduced and then, in 1953, the Power Free was joined by a larger 60 cc model called the Diamond Free. This was still a clip-on unit and retained the 2-speed gear which was improved. The engine unit remained a simple 2-stroke with single vertical cylinder with a separate cylinder head carrying a plug angled to the right.

The crankcase extended back to enclose the transmission and each side cover carried the legend 'Diamond Free' and the words 'Porter Motor'. The engine fitted neatly into the cycle frame and its fuel was carried in a small tank mounted on the frame top tube. It was popular and several thousand were built and sold every month.

SJK Colleda 250 cc twin, the model TT of 1956 with horseshoe style headlamp and Earles forks

Suzuki Two-strokes

The company became known by its initials SJK which stood for Suzuki Jidosha Kogyo or Suzuki Automotive Industries and in 1954 built its first complete motorcycle. It was called the Colleda and this name became used for their machines for several years and viewed as a marque in its own right. The name came from the Japanese expression 'Kore da' which meant 'this one!' and was chosen as a marketing ploy.

It was a major step for Suzuki to go into motorcycle production for the war between Japanese makes was then at its height and he could have more easily continued to just build engine units for others to use. Instead he chose to meet Honda and Tohatsu, the industry leaders, head on and to do this produced a new machine with a new engine.

The 2-stroke cycle was abandoned as too inefficient and unreliable as built in Japan at that date and a single cylinder 4-stroke with overhead valves was used. Engine dimensions were 48 × 50 mm and the resultant 90·5 cc produced 4 bhp at 5000 rpm. A 3-speed gearbox was built in unit with the engine to make a neat package which went into one of two types of frame.

For the commuter or tourer the frame was built up from channel section steel pressings

By 1958 the ST had a pivoted rear fork but was still labelled as a Colleda and made by SJK

18

which added to the weight but kept the cost down and offered strength and durability. For the more sporting customer a tubular frame was used but this version cost more and was not so popular.

In either case the frame was equipped with plunger rear suspension and telescopics at the front. Small drum brakes were used in the wire spoke wheels, the mudguards were fitted close to the tyres and a saddle and rear carrier were provided.

The CO, as it was called, was rather underpowered for its weight but was an innovative model. It was the first Japanese machine to come with a speedometer and one of the few in that era to have automatic ignition advance. In addition maintenance had been much in mind at the design stage so the contact points were mounted outboard of the magneto for easy access and an oil filter was fitted as standard.

To overcome the power deficiency the engine was bored out to give 125 cc and this model became the COX and appeared in 1955. It was however a temporary expedient for at the same time Suzuki launched a completely new model, the ST. This was a 2-stroke and the result of careful thinking by the company engineers who could see no reson why it should not be both as powerful and reliable as a 4-stroke. If they could make it so it had to be cheaper and easier to built and thus Suzuki turned away from 4-strokes for over 20 years.

They became 2-stroke specialists, meeting Yamaha head on, and the ST was their first modern machine with that engine type. It was a single with the classic dimensions of 52×58 mm used by many others before and after it to give a capacity of 123 cc. A 3-speed gearbox was built in unit with the engine which was of straight forward design with iron barrel, light alloy head, four main bearings and a caged roller big end. The electrics were a good deal better than usual for a Japanese machine in 1955 and at first the machine used the CO frame with plunger rear suspension. This proved troublesome so was replaced with a rigid one as it was felt more desirable to be reliable than comfortable if one had to make a choice.

Before long an improved plunger frame was in use and in this form the model sold in substantial numbers along with others. The bicycle clip-on engines had been dropped by the end of 1954 and their place was taken by the MF1 or Mini-Free. This was sold as a complete machine and had the engine unit mounted ahead of the pedalling gear and below the down tube. It was a 50 cc 2-stroke unit which drove the rear wheel directly by a vee belt tensioned with a spring loaded jockey wheel. The fuel tank went on the right alongside the top of the rear wheel and the bicycle pedal chain was also on the right as usual.

The machine was still essentially a bicycle with an engine attached for it retained the bicycle frame and forks although the first was fitted with a spring up rear stand and the second were strutted to deal with the added weight and speed. Saddle, handlebars, mudguards and rear carrier were all bicycle while the brakes were on the rim at the front but with a small drum at the rear. It was a simple, basic machine that held its place in the range until 1958 when a more modern moped took over its job.

The 4-stroke models were completely replaced by late 1955 when the 100 cc Porter Free appeared and the model CO went. The new machine was a smaller version of the ST in a tubular frame and was built for a couple of years. They were still sold as Colleda models and with the SJK initials although the Suzuki Motor Co. Ltd. had come into being in the middle of 1954. It was not until late in 1958 that the stylized S came to be used as a trademark and the machines took their Suzuki name.

Of much more interest than the small singles was the Colleda TT introduced in the middle of 1956 for it was Suzuki's first twin and first machine with a 250 cc engine. It was radically different from the earlier models for it had a pressed steel spine frame, pivoted fork rear suspension and Earles leading link forks at the front. The engine was built in unit with the 4-speed gearbox which had both kickstart lever and rocking pedal gearchange on the left. The final drive chain went on the right and was fully enclosed as was the carburettor and much of the works.

The rear fork was built up from pressings like the main frame but the front one was tubular although the members carrying it were pressings. Full width hubs were used in the wire spoke wheels and each contained a single leading shoe drum brake. The mudguards were both well valanced and sprung so the front one sat well clear of the tyre, a common problem when Earles forks were used and the guard not kept light and unsprung.

At the top of the forks went a massive headlamp with foglamp beneath it and turn indicators on stalks on each side. The headlamp rim was styled into the form of an inverted horseshoe as had been done for some time on the Suzuki machines and which helped to establish brand recognition. In the top of the headlamp cowling went the speedometer and a neutral indicating light. The fuel tank had chrome plated sides and behind it went a single seat with carrier and hand grip on the rear mudguard. Covers went on each side of the main spine beam to enclose the electrics, tools and air filter. The round tank badge carried the Colleda name and the engine side castings the SJK initials. It was apparent that Suzuki had been inspecting the German Adler.

In 1957 the 250 cc twin became the model TP in a revamped frame with twin down tubes which bolted to the front of the engine. At the front went telescopic forks and a neater front mudguard while the full width hubs were retained along with the two low level exhaust systems.

That same year Suzuki commissioned a new factory with automated assembly lines and Michio himself retired, aged 70. He now had plenty of choice of transport if he wanted to go fishing for aside from motorcycles, his firm had begun to build lightweight cars with 360 cc engines as early as 1954.

1958 brought a further step forward and real financial security with the introduction of the Suzumoped SM model, an updated Mini-Free that could be turned out in tens of thousands to provide the commercial base for the company.

The SM came onto the market at the same time as the Honda Supercub step-thru and they both expanded their sales into new markets well removed from the traditional motorcyclist. The Honda provided a new style, a true form of universal transport, while the Suzumoped went more in the direction of the sophisticated European moped. This had developed on from the days of the clip-on and models such as the NSU Quickly with its simple controls and 2- or 3-speed gearbox had become extremely popular.

The Suzumoped used the engine unit from the Mini-Free installed in a spine frame with short leading-link front forks and a pivoted fork at the rear. Unlike the NSU, and the Honda, there was no question of the machine being a step-thru as a conventional petrol tank went forward of the single seat. The frame spine ran straight back from the headstock to the top of the rear unit with an extension down behind the engine to support it, the rear fork and the pedalling gear. Final drive was still by belt on the left which was adequate and gave a quiet smooth transmission.

Not for long however for when the Mark II appeared it had chain drive and with this it ran on to mature into a miniature motorcycle with gearbox, kickstart, full chaincase and normal centre-stand. It retained the cantilever sprung saddle, copied from the Germans, with carrier behind it on the rear mudguard and gradually assumed a more sporting profile.

Alongside it came the Selped series which had much in common with spine frame, leading links, pivoted rear and single saddle but in a format more like that of the Honda Cub. The use of a fuel tank above the engine reduced the drop of the frame so the step-thru feature was not as obvious as on the Honda but it was there and the model came with legshields so fitted the same market section.

By 1960 a 4-speed gearbox was used on the Selped along with an electric starter and an electro-magnetic cold start on the carburettor.

All devices that helped to make the model more acceptable to lady riders and the vast, non-technical, commuter market. Less successful was an electro-magnetic clutch and that model had a very short life.

During 1959 the 125 cc single cylinder ST model was replaced by two twins. By then the single had moved on both in design and styling with the engine hung from a spine frame, telescopics still at the front, pivoted fork at the rear and electric start. A single seat and rear carrier

The 1959 Colleda Seltwin SB of 125 cc

The Suzumoped introduced in 1958 using the Mini-Free engine in a spine frame. Original belt drive soon gave way to chain seen on this 1959 example

were still fitted, the rear chain was fully enclosed and the styling was 'jet age'. This had the headlamp built into a nacelle formed at the top of the forks and which also carried the instruments. The tank sides carried chrome side panels bearing the stylized S and their form was run down and back into the side panels. The styling lines were rather heavy and mainly straight but overall the effect was similar to that of the early 1980s but without the finishing run into seat base and tail unit.

In place of the old style singles came a number of models that showed the lines for the future range. They were in both sports and touring forms but with a new and lighter appearance. The smallest was the R50 and this was a very sporting machine that ran to 11000 rpm to produce its 7 bhp which were transmitted through a 5-speed gearbox. A spine frame carried the engine unit and was fitted with leading link front forks and a tank line very changed from that of the Colleda models.

The MD was very similar but of 52 cc and cast in the touring mould with a lower engine speed so it could manage with four speeds. It retained the leading links at the front with a heavier style mudguard to suit its more staid gait.

The 125 cc SH model continued with the Colleda lines and was a continuation of the ST series with its spine frame. The 80K which came in 1962 was very different and on the lines of the R50

The Selped MA from 1960 with the stylized Suzuki S on engine and tank

but with an 80 cc engine, a 4-speed gearbox and telescopic front forks. From it came a whole string of machines in various sizes and layouts right into the 1980s.

Back in 1959 the new machine was called the Seltwin and came in 125 and 150 cc sizes with similar but more pronounced styling. The engines were much as the 250 with slightly inclined, parallel cylinders, twin low level exhaust pipes and silencers, cowled carburettors behind the barrels and unit construction of engine and gearbox. The rear chain went on the left, opposite to the single, and the spine frame was fitted with telescopic front forks styled to retain the appearance of leading links at their lower ends. The saddle was a block that filled the space behind the tank and above the side covers while the rear carrier with its grab rail was retained.

The Seltwin was supplied complete with legshields and proved very popular with younger riders. It ran on in various guises into 1963 and it was not until late in its life that its appearance changed to any extent. Then the tank and side covers were styled into separate rectangles set as the opposed segments of a divided square in line with the other models in the range. At the same time the silencers lengthened and were cut off at their ends without tailpipes while at the front the forks became telescopic in appearance. The front mudguard became unsprung so fitted neatly round the tyre and the headlamp shell became smaller and held to fork shroud ears although it still carried the speedometer. By this time it had progressed from being the SB model to the SL via a variety of letters.

Along with the 125, the 250 cc twin continued and for 1960 became the Colleda Twinace or TA with styling akin to the Seltwin. Many of the features were on the same lines, one common one being the mounting of the rear units. On the chain side the lower end was level with the top of the chaincase and thus, to match, the other fork arm was extended up. To accommodate the feature and retain the unit length meant the top fixings being well up and level with the rear carrier. Telescopics were fitted at the front styled to retain the leading link look as on the 125 twin along with the heavily valanced, sprung mudguard and this was matched at the rear.

A 250 cc twin on test, the 1962 model TB with spine frame, telescopics and discreetly styled headlamp

The most novel feature of the machine was the coupled hydraulic braking system. Both wheels had single leading shoe drum brakes and the foot pedal operated a master cylinder connected to both. The braking effect was set in a ratio between front and rear after extensive tests and a normal hand lever was connected to the front by cable to supplement the hydraulics. It was a good idea and not dissimilar in principle to that of the later Moto Guzzi but failed to catch public acceptance so was abandoned.

In 1962 the 250 became the TB and then the TC in 1963 with a number of styling changes and some mechanical ones. The engine stayed as it

was with the twin Mikuni carburettors, Amals made under licence, under a cover and the long silencers, one on each side. The 4-speed gearbox was driven by helical gears and built in unit with the engine and the assembly hung from a spine frame as before. The legshields were left off and their absence helped to make the machine look lighter.

This aspect was helped by a change to normal telescopics at the front with an unsprung front mudguard replacing the earlier heavy affair. The headlamp shell was made separate but still carried the speedometer while the front brake was cable operated. The rear one continued with its master cylinder and hydraulic mechanism.

The engine had a dynamo that doubled as an electric starter fixed to the left end of the crankshaft and the primary drive on the right. Ignition was by coil and lubrication by petroil mix while a kickstart lever and mechanism were retained as a precaution. However Suzuki confidence relegated the lever to the toolbox and it was only attached to its spindle if needed. The gearbox was typical of many Japanese of the period in that the selection cam was able to fully rotate and thus the rider could change from top to neutral to bottom, a feature hardly conducive to road safety or a happy engine. The advantage of being able to stop in top gear and move straight to neutral was hardly worth the attendant risks.

The styling changed and became lighter with a new fuel tank, with built in fuel gauge in the form of an outside level pipe, and different side covers. A dualseat went in place of the single seat and a carrier went behind that over the end of the rear mudguard. This carried a useful, horizontal tail to keep road spray away from the rider and whitewall tyres were fitted.

With 50, 125 and 250 cc models, Suzuki were into real mass production and in a position to challenge Honda. However they chose to diversify more into small cars which ate up production capacity so they stayed at number two of the motorcycle makers.

They had exported in a small way as far back as 1952 and at first concentrated on SE Asia and then Africa. Gradually the list of countries expanded and the numbers built up so by the end of the decade they had the experience to move further afield. It was a time to expand as the home market had changed from expansion to replacement and new sales areas were needed to support production plans.

Rear view of same 250 cc TB which shows the reservoir for the hydraulic rear brake and the full chaincase

1963 was the turning point when Suzuki changed up a gear or two and went into the American, English and Australian markets. In each case the beginnings were small but quickly built up. In Europe the Suzuki reputation had jumped forward with success in 50 cc road racing championships and then the 125. In England there was an early association with the AMC group but when they failed Suzuki(GB) came to be and in 1969 joined forces with the Lambretta Trojan group headed by Peter Agg. In time they moved to Croydon, just south of London, and later to Crawley, close to Gatwick Airport while in 1975 they became part of the vast Heron group.

In the USA the firm set up office in California to serve the large west coast market and later opened branch offices across that vast country. Australia followed this pattern with a distributor in each state and in Central and South America, plus Canada the Suzuki S moved in.

Before 1963 Suzuki were like many Japanese motorcycle firms. They copied, they experimented, they went up blind alleys and they established their basic business. They fought to stay solvent through the traumatic 1950s and they had won through.

After 1963 the struggles would continue but in a different key, to a different background and on a much bigger scale. Suzuki moved into action with a new model and one that set a theme for the mid-1960s.

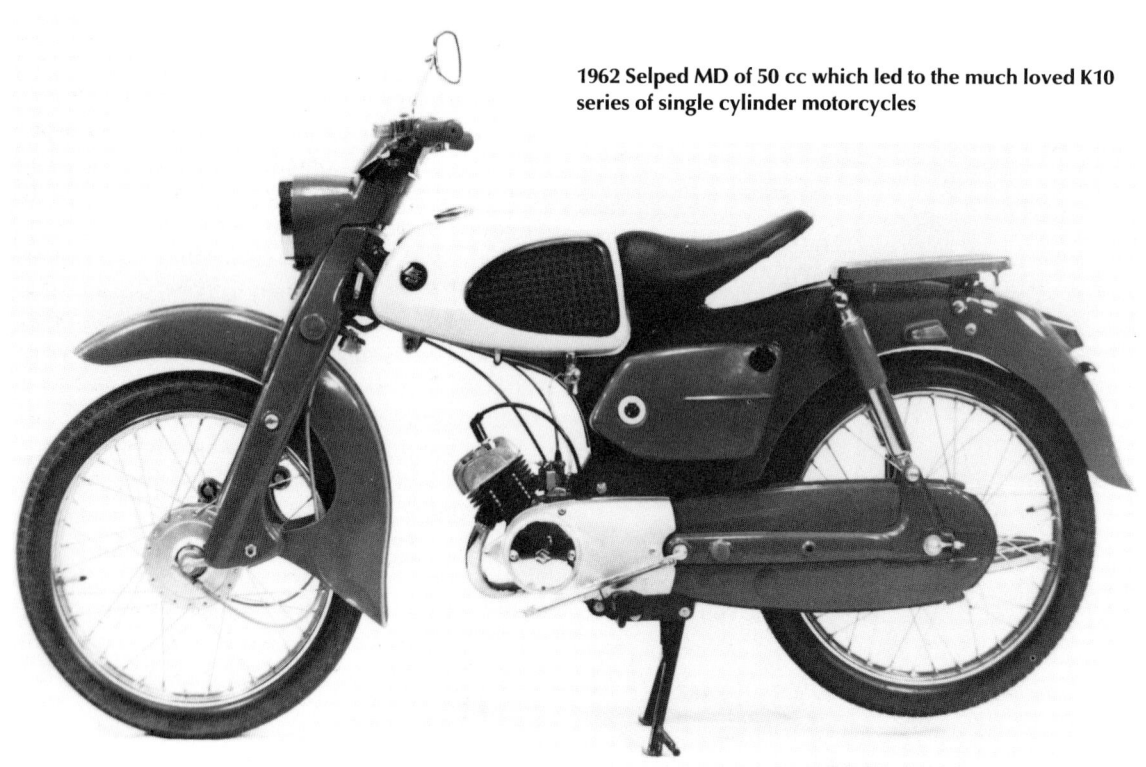

1962 Selped MD of 50 cc which led to the much loved K10 series of single cylinder motorcycles

2 | Road singles

When Suzuki launched their 80 cc Selped model K10 in 1962 they set a new theme in Japanese motorcycling where riders were becoming tired of their 50 cc machines. As was usual all over the world they craved something bigger and faster which is precisely what Suzuki gave them.

An 80 cc engine size may seem small when viewed from the saddle of a 500 but to the rider of a moped it meant a 60 per cent increase. In addition the Suzuki was well engineered to produce 7·5 bhp at 6500 rpm which gave the machine a claimed top speed of 56 mph, a very useful figure in Japan in the early 1960s.

The K10 engine was based on dimensions of 45 × 50 mm and a capacity of 79·5 cc. It was a straight forward 2-stroke with piston controlled ports and had its cylinder inclined forward a little from the vertical. Both cylinder head and barrel were cast in aluminium, the latter sleeved, and the actual compression ratio was 6·7:1. The carburettor tucked in behind the cylinder under a shield and the exhaust ran low down on the right. Lubrication was by petroil and ignition by flywheel magneto, this assembly also incorporating the generator which supplied power for the lights and battery.

The 4-speed gearbox was built in unit with the engine and driven by primary gears and a wet clutch. It was of cross-over type with the output sprocket on the left and the foot pedal went on the same side. As was normal at that time, neutral was above first gear and selected by a

Above **The Selped K10 model in 1962, an 80 cc machine with four-speed gearbox and full equipment**

Right **A K11 sports Suzuki being presented against an interesting background touching on the firm's racing successes**

full movement of the pedal. The kickstart pedal went on the right and drove direct to the crankshaft to enable the engine to be easily started even if a gear was engaged.

The engine unit went into an updated version of the moped spine frame with an added support tube bolted in between the front of the crankcase and the bottom of the headstock. At the front went telescopic forks with shrouds over the suspension springs while the rear wheel was carried in a pivoted fork. Both wheels had full width, light alloy hubs with drum brakes and were built up with wire spokes and steel rims. Whitewall tyres were available as an option along with legshields, windscreen, mirrors and alternative sprockets for rear wheel or gearbox.

The first models were fitted with the Colleda style of tank and cantilever saddle plus rear carrier but the last two items were soon replaced by a dualseat and the style of the tank and the side covers evolved year by year.

The K10 was an immediate success in Japan and was soon being exported. In 1963 it was joined by a sports version, the K11, which had both engine and cycle part changes. The engine was improved to increase its power to 8·0 bhp at 7500 rpm while the appearance was changed with a raised exhaust system that ran back on the right at crankcase top level. Suspension springs front and rear were exposed, although the fronts later gained protective gaiters, and a short, narrow front mudguard was fitted, supported by cross stays. Straight handlebars were supplied and Suzuki had another winner.

That same year also saw the introduction of four 50 cc models, three much on the lines of the 80's. The base machine was the M15 which was essentially as the K10 except for the lack of

The K10P in 1967 with the benefit of an oil pump and a Selmix label on the oil tank

bracing downtube and the fitment of leading link front forks. The engine design was similar to that of the larger model but the details and parts differed so one was not a bored or stroked version of the other.

The M15 engine had dimensions of 41 × 38 mm, a capacity of 50 cc, compression ratio of 6·7:1 and power output of 4·2 bhp at 8000 rpm. It was petroil lubricated and built in unit with a 4-speed gearbox of different ratios to the K10. As with all the models of that era, the rear chain was fully enclosed.

The second 50 was the M15D which was essentially the same except for the addition of a starter-dynamo, 12 volt electrics and coil ignition. That model looked after the luxury end of the market and the third machine, the M12, catered for the sportsman. It followed the lines of the K11 with raised exhaust and was fitted with telescopic front forks, narrow front mudguard, dualseat and exposed suspension springs.

The final model was completely different for it was a step-thru moped aimed directly at the Honda Cub. Honda gave the customer 4-stroke power, Suzuki used a 2-stroke but otherwise the two models had much in common. The Suzuki, called the M30, had an inclined engine with piston controlled porting and dimensions of 41 × 38 mm. Compression ratio was 6·3:1 and power produced 4 bhp at 6800 rpm while lubrication was petroil and ignition by flywheel magneto.

The engine was built in unit with a 3-speed gearbox which it drove via an automatic clutch.

This contained a transmission shock absorber in its centre and was driven from the crankshaft by a pair of helical gears, the larger one of which was rivetted to the clutch drum. The plates inside this were brought into contact by the centrifugal action of a ring of ball bearings which flew out as the drum speeded up. The gears were controlled by a pedal on the left and the engine started with a kickstarter on the right which meshed via the back of the clutch gear to give primary starting.

The frame was typical step-thru with the main beam running down from the headstock to a point just above the engine. The central area enclosed the carburettor and electrical items and the frame then swept up and back over the rear wheel. Pivoted fork rear suspension was provided, side covers enclosed the battery and tools and the fuel tank bolted to the top of the frame. In this position it supported the front of the dualseat which ran back onto the top of the rear mudguard section of the frame.

At the front went leading link forks and a typical step-thru plastic front mudguard, light and extensive. Both wheels had drum brakes and wire spokes and the engine was cowled in by large legshields.

The headlamp, which like all the Suzuki ones was still of a horseshoe shape, was built into the top of the fork assembly with the speedometer set in its top and turn indicators and rear view mirrors were provided. A rear carrier was available as was a windscreen and thus Suzuki had a model they could offer against the Cub. In 1965 they added a 4-speed 80 cc version called the M80 for riders seeking a little more power.

1964 brought two more machines, both a little larger than the others already in the range. Both were nominally in the 125 cc class, both were to remain in production in one form or another

50 cc version of the small motorcycle, an M15 built 1963–67 and much as the K series

for many years and both were very popular.

The first was the S10 which in some ways had its roots in the older Colleda models but updated for the mid sixties. The second was the B100, actually a 120, which used a different engine form in similar cycle parts.

The S10 engine had dimensions of 54 × 54 mm and a capacity of 124 cc. It breathed through a disc valve on the right and exhausted into twin pipes with a low set silencer on each side of the machine. The cylinder was cast in iron which was unusual for a Suzuki but the head was light alloy as normal. A 4-speed gearbox was built in unit with the engine with gear pedal and final drive on the left and kickstarter on the right and, despite the disc valve, the whole unit had a rather old fashioned air to it.

Not so the B100 which had an engine on the lines of the K10 but with dimensions of 52 × 56 mm and a capacity of 119 cc. Power output was 10 bhp at 7000 rpm on a compression ratio of 7·2:1 and this came from a conventional piston controlled port layout. The cylinder was in light alloy with a sleeve, the head aluminium.

A 4-speed gearbox was built in unit with the engine but both its internal ratios and those of the primary and final drives differed from those of the S10. Unlike that model the B100 had a single exhaust pipe and silencer low down on the right and as on the smaller singles had its carburettor hidden by a cover.

Both the S10 and the B100 had spine frames, telescopic front forks, pivoted forks at the rear, full width drum brakes, dualseats, and many

Left **Suzukis such as this M12 were handled by AMC early on. This 50 cc machine was a good seller**

Below **Typical Suzuki single, this a TS250 with oil pump, 5-speed gearbox and conventional construction**

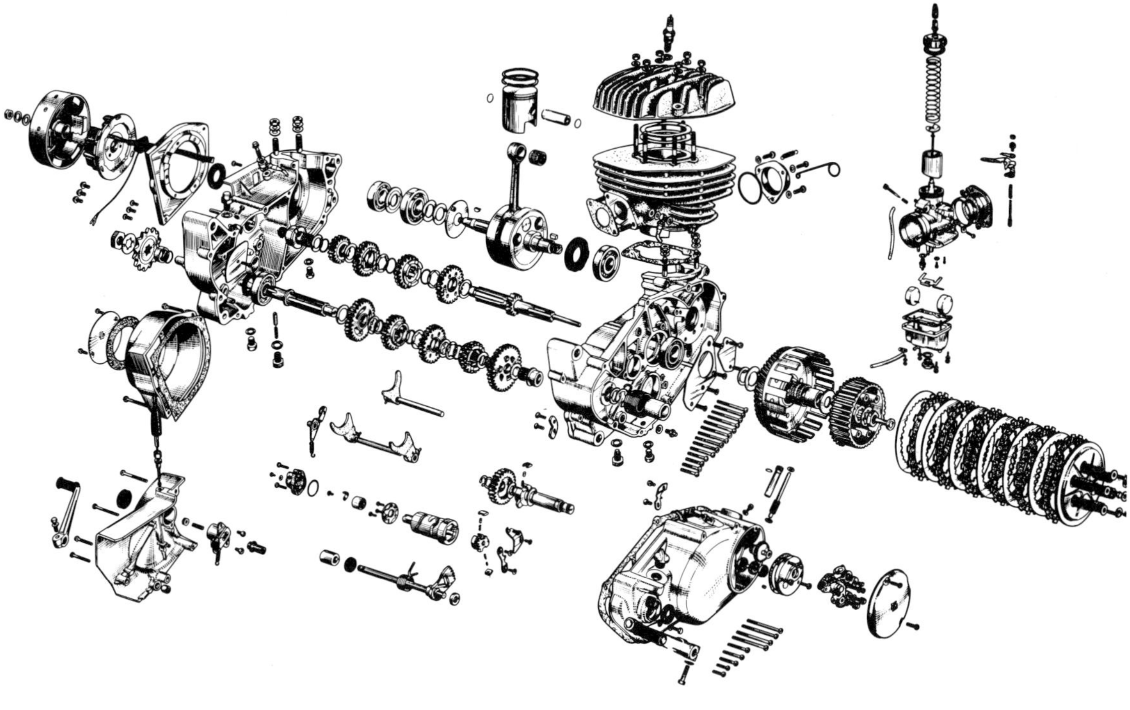

Road singles

33

Above **The Suzuki step-thru, the M30 with 2-stroke engine and 3-speed gearbox with automatic clutch**

Right **The B100P of 1966 with Posi-Force lubrication and comprehensive specification. Very popular commuter machine**

other items of similar type. A noted difference was the fitment of a bracing downtube on the S10 but there were many others. The speedometer drive was from the right on the S10 and the left, brake backplate, side on the B100. Front mudguards were heavy or light, the tanks were a different shape as were the bars and overall the two machines looked most dissimilar.

And so they stayed, both of them, throughout very long production runs. The S10 became the K125 in 1967 and was invariably finished in black with silver tank panels and with its smaller 16 in. wheels became the unexciting workhorse that thousands used to get to work and go shopping with. Such models formed the backbone of a successful company.

The B100 was brighter, usually with a colour finish and chromed or stainless front mudguard

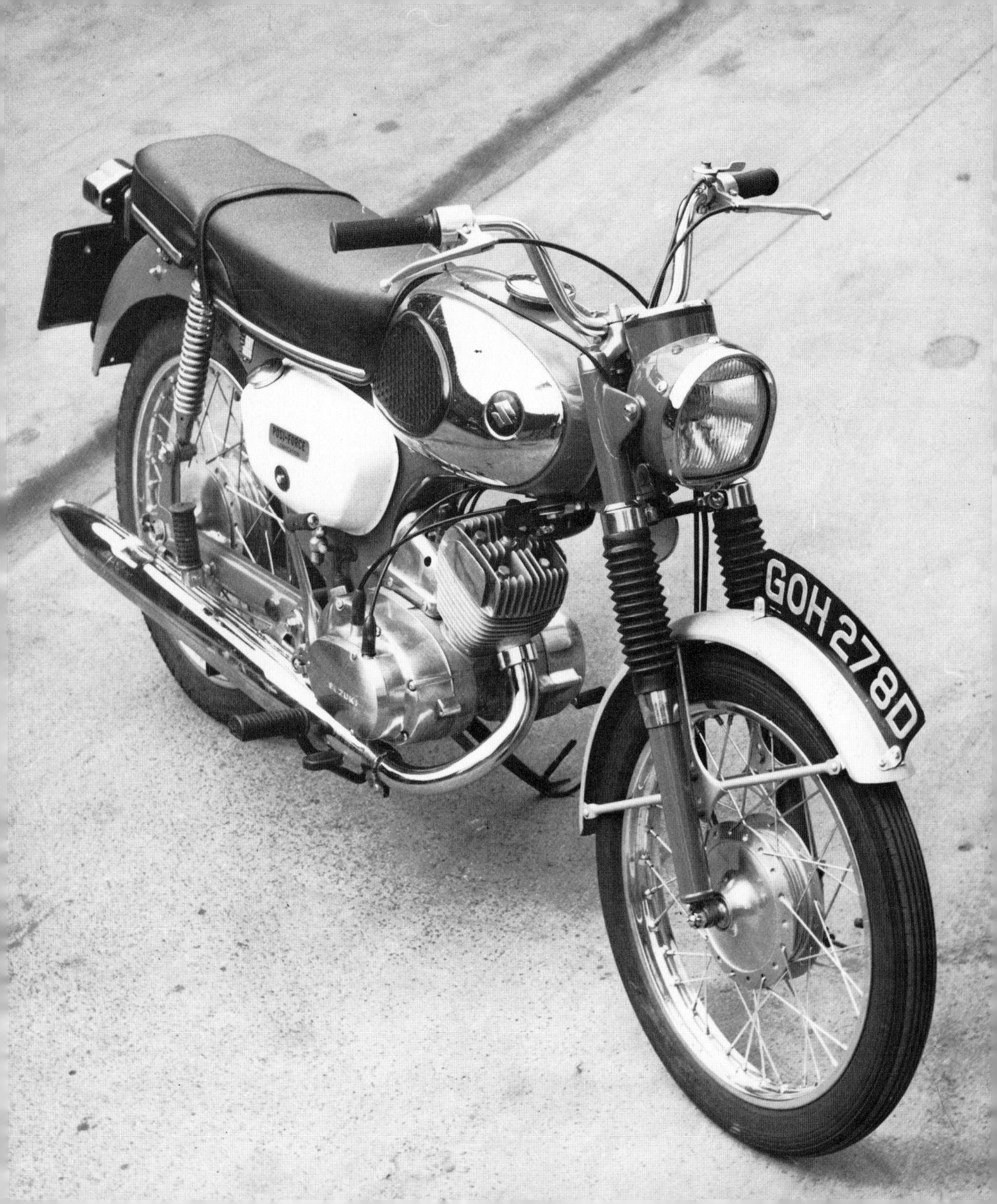
POSI-FORCE
GOH 278D

Suzuki Two-strokes

The very basic K125 in 1976 still with its twin exhausts. Disc valve, four speeds and iron barrel

Left **The lubrication system showing the pump, the link to the throttle, the check valve and the big-end feed**

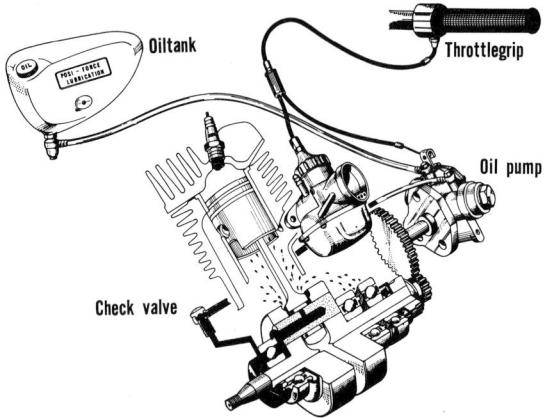

plus chromed tank panels. It ran on slightly bigger 17 in. wheels that were shod with narrower tyres which with the light front mudguard gave it a more sporting look.

As the midpoint of the decade slipped by many Suzuki models took a big step forward with a change in their lubrication system. Petroil mixing was a nuisance and not even cheap. It was technically poor as it had to have enough oil to cope with full throttle loads at very low engine speeds and thus was over-oiled for the rest of the time.

The answer was an oil pump with a variable output governed by both engine speed and throttle position. It was a system adopted by all the Japanese in time and proved most effective for road machines with their widely varying engine loads and speeds. Suzuki called their arrangement Posi-force and pumped the oil through one main bearing into a catch disc which fed the big end rollers. By the early seventies the name had changed to Controlled Crankshaft Injection or Suzuki CCI and had completely replaced the old notion of mixing petrol and oil.

To distinguish the addition of the oil pump which was normally crankshaft driven, the letter P was added to the model typing to give K10P, K11P and B100P, the last becoming the 'bloop' in the UK at least although elsewhere it was renamed the B120. During the same period the M series began to come to an end but not before the M15 had appeared in a Mark II form with telescopic front forks.

1967 brought a new model in the form of the A100 and one that was to run on virtually unchanged until 1980 although at first it was only sold on the home, Japanese market. The single cylinder was inclined well forward, so far in fact that the fins ran along its length and matched similar ones on each side of the head. Both head and barrel were in light alloy, the latter with an iron sleeve, and engine dimensions were square at 50 mm to give a capacity of 98 cc. Compression ratio was 6·5:1 and induction via a disc valve on the right which helped the engine produce 9·5 bhp at 7500 rpm. The exhaust ran low down on the right side, ignition was by flywheel magneto and lubrication by pump using the CCI system.

A 4-speed gearbox was built in unit with the engine and driven by a helical gear primary and multi-plate clutch. The gears were all in-direct and the box of the cross-over design with the output sprocket on the left. A primary kickstart

The later B120 version of the B100. Little changed but the oil system is now called CCI

Suzuki Two-strokes

was used and the rear chain was fully enclosed.

The engine unit was mounted in a spine frame with telescopic front forks and pivoted fork rear suspension. The frame was built up from pressings with the oil tank for the CCI on the right and a cover on the left to conceal the battery, tools and electrics. A large round air cleaner went above the engine unit and clipped to the crankcase which had an internal passage to the carburettor. The wheels had full width drum brakes and wire spokes and separate mudguards were fitted front and rear. The front was narrow

The A100 built for many years with few changes. Disc valve, drum air cleaner and special finning

with a single cross-stay on each side and the rear deeper with a valance to stiffen it. At its rear went a small horizontal mud flap.

The fuel tank had kneegrips and chrome side panels, the speedometer was set in the top of the headlamp shell, a dualseat was provided along with passenger footrests and the machine was fitted with turn indicators.

It was a successful format and was quickly

repeated in a smaller capacity to give the A50 which ran on until the late seventies. The format was the same with near horizontal cylinder, disc valve, spine frame and all the other features of the A100. Engine dimensions were 41 × 37·8 mm to give a capacity of 49·9 cc, compression ratio was 6·7:1 and power produced 4·9 bhp at 8500 rpm.

The main differences lay in the gearbox, which had five speeds, and the engine oil pump drive although both models had the pump located in the same place behind the gearbox sprocket. It was driven from the gear the kickstart mechanism engaged with and on the A50, this meshed with a free running gear on the output shaft which in turn meshed with one cut on the mainshaft. The net result was that if the rider had the machine in gear and the clutch disengaged the pump was no longer driven. In the A100 a separate pair of gears took the drive from the back of the clutch drum to the pump so the problem did not arise but the space they occupied was taken up by the added gear in the 50. It never seemed to worry the many thousands produced.

Having established a style and form that the customers liked and which sold well Suzuki proceeded to ring the changes with it. One of the

An A100 in 1972. Revised tank and side cover styling cloak unaltered mechanics

Suzuki Two-strokes

Left **The U50 step-thru of 1966–68 which replaced the M30 and became the F50**

Far left **1977 model A100 with dancer Perdita Hobart. Machine styling again revised but mechanics the same**

Below **The F50 step-thru of 1969–73 which took over from the U50. Still three speeds and leading links**

Road singles

41

Above **The FR70, the final step-thru form built in both this 70 cc and a 50 cc size**

Left **The M50 moped built from 1969–77 with trailing link forks and basic specification**

Right **The AS50 of 1968–70, a sports model with humped back seat and raised exhaust**

first was the AS50 which was a sports version. Thus it had the exhaust system raised and run along the left side with a perforated heat shield attached to the silencer. The full chaincase became a chainguard, the front forks received gaiters and the seat, tank and finish were changed to a more sporting style. It was popular and sold well.

Along with the 50 and 100 models came a 90 cc series. This began in 1967 with the A90 and single seat K90, both using the same disc valve engine with 4-speed gearbox. The A90 was short lived but was joined by variants with sports fittings, high or low exhaust pipes and bigger wheels during 1968, these having AS or AC prefixes and a G suffix on occasion. The K90 ran to 1969 and then had a revised engine fitted to continue as the K90G for a year or two and then as the K90 again to 1976. For 1967 there had also been a K80 on the same lines. As these new models appeared, so production of the older K series was brought to a halt. The old M30 and M80 went with the other M series and in their place in 1966 came the U50 and U70 which were both step-thru's in the same style but with disc valve engines. That aside, they repeated the lead-

Road singles

43

Left **One of the family, the A80 of 1972–76 in familiar format of disc valve and spine frame**

Below **Two sports hundreds, the ASS100 on the left with low exhaust and ACC100 with raised pipe**

ing link forks, pressed steel frames and legshields typical of the type.

In 1969 these were superceded by the F50 and F70 models which continued the same theme with near horizontal cylinders but with reed valves set in the right side of the crankcase so they had all the appearance of the disc valve layout. They continued with the automatic clutch and 3-speed gearbox controlled by a foot pedal on the left, flywheel magneto ignition and oil pump lubrication.

While the step-thru style remained the same the execution changed. The frame still swept down and then up again but with the fuel tank

The 1974 model A50 in the stock Suzuki single format, and very successful too

in a new position and more support for the dualseat. The suspension remained the same but the legshields became a one piece moulding while the rear mudguard become separate.

In 1974 the models became the FR50 and FR70 with cosmetic changes to the chassis. The rear mudguard became part of the frame and the front mudguard altered in shape a trifle. The seat and side covers were altered but the essentials stayed as they were as regards engine, gearbox, suspension and brakes.

The two models ran on to 1976 and were then both replaced by the FR80, simply the same medicine as before with a slightly bigger engine. Otherwise it retained all the well tried features that stemmed back to the first M30. With styling changes it rolled on into the eighties still doing the same job of providing basic transport.

In 1969 the step-thru's had been joined by a simpler model, the M50 moped with 50 cc engine and 2-speed gearbox. This went into a simple tube frame and while the rear suspension was as usual, that at the front was by small trailing links. Otherwise it was fitted out as expected with saddle, rear carrier and front basket. It also had a front apron which came back to partially enclose the engine and was a successful machine that stayed in production into the late seventies. In 1970 the step-thru range was augmented by a 90 cc model which varied a little from the others in that the front suspension was by trailing links but of a more substantial nature than on the M50. Wheel size was smaller than usual at 2·75 × 14 in. but in other respects the model followed the step-thru pattern.

The approach of the seventies saw a number

of variations of the basic machines appearing including a new engine size in the form of the A70 in 1967, following its first appearance the year before is the K30. This followed the lines of the A100 with a 4-speed gearbox and ran until 1972 before becoming the slightly larger A80. Both followed the A100 format very closely and the first had engine dimensions of 46 × 42 mm, a capacity of 69·8 cc, 7·0:1 compression ratio and produced 7·5 bhp at 7500 rpm. The A80 was produced by boring out to 47 mm which increased the capacity to 72·9 cc and raised the power a trifle to 7·7 bhp. In this form it ran on to 1976.

In the 100 cc class two sports models appeared for 1970, these being the ASS100 which had its exhaust system low down on the right and the ACC100 which had a raised system on the left with a heat shield attached. Both models differed from the basic A100 in tank, seat, mudguards, handlebars and finish and both had gaitered forks. A chainguard replaced the chaincase and this item and the mudguards could be obtained with a chrome plated finish to give models with a suffix letter G after their names. They were only made for a year or two as the fashions in small sports machines moved on.

The 50 cc A50 lost its sports version AS50 in 1970 but gained two other cousins, the AC50 and the K50. The first had been listed since 1969 and was essentially the AS model with another name and repeated that machine's raised exhaust on the left, gaitered forks and seat styled to give a hint of road racing. It was a popular option for anyone who wanted their 50 cc motorcycle to look a little different and sold well until withdrawn around 1976. From 1973 the basic A50 was also available as the GA50 with the addition of engine protection bars running from headstock to footrests.

The second model dated from 1967 but was aimed at a very different sector for it was a rock bottom, no frills machine. It used the reed valve engine and from 1970 on a 3-speed gearbox, after early years with a 4-speed one, all in the A50 chassis package. Like the 125 cc K125 it came in black with silver tank panels and had well valanced mudguards and a full chaincase to match its sober finish. Useful items such as kneegrips on the tank sides were included so many preferred it to the more flashy models. It ran on happily to 1976 along with the K125 which had gained an oil pump but otherwise continued with little change. For 1967 the 50 cc model was also offered in sports form as the KS50 but was soon replaced by the AS version.

The other 125, the B100P, became the B120 in the UK in 1970 with the same simple, reliable engine and really not much change to the chassis. There were detail alternations to the tank, seat and graphics but otherwise the change from gaiters to shrouds for the front fork was the most noticed. Just as one would expect with such a model. In 1975 it became the B120S or Student but otherwise ran on as basic transport in place of the K125 for three years. At the end of its time the only real difference between it and the first B100 was the oil pump added to the engine.

In 1975 a new model appeared especially built for the UK market. At that time youngsters of sixteen were restricted to mopeds and had to wait until seventeen before sampling the delights of motorcycling up to 250 cc as learners. The UK definition of a moped was then a machine of under 50 cc fitted with pedalling gear and based on machines such as the old NSU Quickly and the later Puch Maxi.

The latter was very popular but was essentially a light machine with open rigid frame and rather crude telescopic front forks. It relied much on its excellent saddle for rider comfort and was essentially a development of the clip-on model. Its top speed was around 30 mph but few kept to this after a mile as it became too lively and

Right **The A50P built from 1975–77 with pedals to suit UK laws. Dropped when legal moped specification changed**

The 1976 AC50 with stylish seat and raised black exhaust system

1976 GT100 with more upright engine, tubular frame and disc front brake

Road singles

GT50 from 1978 but still fitted with pedals. New style of machine in line with trends for the eighties

20–25 mph was its usual gait.

It was this machine which sold in large numbers, and others like it, that the politicians and bureaucrats envisaged when they drew up the legislation to restrict sixteen year olds to mopeds with scant regard for their wishes. A sixteen year old did not have a vote but he did want a motorcycle with more power, more speed and above all more style. The Japanese industry rallied to the call and quickly produced what became known as sixteener specials and the new Suzuki, the A50P, was one such special.

In essence it was the A50 with pedalling gear but introduced with two features that made it an instant hit with the young. The first was an engagement lever that went on top of the crankcase and enabled the rider to select pedal or engine drive. The mechanism for this was a dog clutch on the gearbox output shaft that either engaged the pedal chain sprocket or left it free while the shaft drove the rear wheel in the normal fashion with a drive chain further inboard.

The pedals went on a shaft that ran across the machine in bushes set in the pivoted fork arms. A sprocket on the left was connected by chain to that on the gearbox shaft so that when the dog clutch was engaged rotation of the pedals drove via the chain to the shaft and thence to the rear wheel by the drive chain. Provided the gearbox was in neutral the rider could thus propel the machine as required by law.

A cover enclosed the pedal chain and by placing the cross-shaft well back the pedals could turn without hitting any of the foot controls. The kickstarter arm was special to the model as it had to curl under the pedal shaft but the brake and gearchange levers were normal. In practice it was none too easy to pedal the machine along due to the relative positions of pedals and handlebars but the arrangements satisfied the legal needs.

The second feature that completely sold the idea to the sixteen year old lay in the design of the pedal shaft. This was contrived so that instead of having to ride with one foot forward and the other to the rear, as on a bicycle and in a fashion that would have made it impossible to brake and change gear at the same time, both pedal arms could point forward and lock in this position to act as normal footrests, albeit with rotating pedals. All the sixteener specials that sold well had this feature and it made a mockery of the legal definition for essentially the moped became a 50 cc sports motorcycle. In place of the 30 mph of the Puch was 50 mph with acceptable acceleration.

It could not last and was an odd situation for the sixteen year old could and did buy his sports model but could not ride his parent's FR50 as it lacked the pedals essential for the moped definition. During 1977 the law changed and a moped became a machine of less than 50 cc capacity with a design speed of 30 mph.

This stopped the production of new sixteener specials in its tracks but the trade in second hand ones flourished. But not for long as they had a hard life and high mortality rate so in a few years nearly all had gone from the scene. Gone but not forgotten by the fortunate youths who were the right age at the right time.

So the A50P went and as the decade drew to its end the range of road singles using the 2-stroke engine changed. In most cases the new models looked forward but one, the GT100 did this for its chassis but went back for the engine unit. It was also unusual in being based on a trail bike for normally it worked the other way with the trail versions being developed using an existing road engine.

This aspect aside the GT100 was a conventional single with disc valve and 5-speed gearbox. As was to be expected it had pump lubrication but unlike the A100 the cylinder was only slightly inclined from the vertical and the engine went into a tubular frame. The front forks were without gaiters and the rear suspension springs were exposed while the front brake was a single disc with hydraulic operation. For the rest it was a conventional small road machine which in a year or so was superceded by the GP series in 100 and 125 cc forms.

Meanwhile, in 1977, a restricted A50 appeared in the UK for the moped market but this area soon saw other models built to the legal needs in attempts to win customers at sixteen in the hope to keep them throughout their motorcycling career.

With the top speed restricted all the machines performed much the same whether in road or off-road format. Thus style and price became the determining factors to the buyer and 50s appeared with disc brakes, cast alloy wheels and other competition orientated features. To cater for all tastes makers produced road models, trail models and even a chopper style with low-rider features of special seat, extended forks and high but laid back bars.

The rest of the road singles in 100 and 125 cc sizes and the scooters, scooterettes and step-thrus all reflected the mood and engineering style of the 1980s but most could see their roots stretching well back to the first K and M models. Environmental needs brought in 4-strokes in smaller sizes but the simple 2-stroke, developed over the years, fulfilled its role so well it was hard to dispense with.

So in small sizes but large numbers they rolled on into the eighties.

3 Off-road singles

The Suzuki off-road machines were developed from road models in the early years but as they became more sophisticated the link between the two became less apparent. In the end they were purpose designed and while a family of off-road models could be related to a single engine unit, the tie-up with a road machine lapsed.

So, early on, a trail bike came from a road model and was built with limited changes but in time could evolve into motocross, enduro, desert and trials machines while the road version would vanish from the range.

One of the earliest off-road models was the K11T which was based on the K11. The main changes were to the fuel tank, tyres and mudguards for the standard engine, frame and forks were used. Competition number plates were added in ISDT form above the headlamp and either side of the rear mudguard tail but the seat and headlamp assembly were standard. High rise bars with a brace were fitted and the chaincase was retained.

Next on the scene was the B105P based on the early B100 plus oil pump, and suitable tyres and mudguards for trail riding. It was aimed at the USA market and while the engine was the normal 119 cc unit the gearbox was very different for in place of the usual four gears were two sets of three, one high for road use and the other low for the trail.

Suzuki contrived to get this assembly with a total of six speeds into the same space with a cunning design and were to go on to use the same idea in at least five other models over the years.

What they did was to couple a 3-speed box with a 2-speed box and arrange the gear ratios so they had three low and three high. As it came out, the ratio for top in the low range was only slightly above bottom in the high range so the rider had five alternative ratios available but in two sets of three.

The detail design retained the all-indirect cross-over arrangement so the drive came into the box on one shaft from the right and exited on the other shaft out to the left. There were four gears on each shaft and the three to the right were laid out as in a 3-speed gearbox. Thus the middle gear on the input shaft could slide to the left to engage top gear and a dog slid between first and second gears on the output shaft to select them.

The fourth gear pair on the left, worked with the one next to it to provide the 2-speed gearbox so one gear pair did duty in both boxes. The two end gears on the input shaft were made in one to run freely on the shaft. The end gear on the output also ran free but on a separate sprocket shaft that carried the gearbox sprocket and ran free in the output shaft. This sprocket shaft was cross-drilled with ball bearings set in the resulting holes and these balls could be pushed out proud of the shaft surface by a plunger rod. The balls engaged with either end gear, to lock in the extra gear reduction, or top gear on the output shaft to give a direct drive.

The plunger rod worked in a hole bored into the sprocket shaft from the left and was enlarged at the end so it forced the balls out as it moved in or out. The larger diameter was of a length that it only moved one set of balls at a time and so by moving in or out one or other gear was obtained. The actual selections was done using a lever mounted external to the gearbox outboard of the drive chain and riders soon became adept at moving this with their left foot rather than by hand. In fact the handbook did suggest kicking the lever until it shifted with a click, it did not give a procedure if it went snap.

The 80 cc model was replaced by the K15 which was similar but used tank, seat and forks from the M15, a sprung, trail type front mudguard, universal tyres and came with rear carrier mounted aft of its rather short dualseat. It retained the raised exhaust system on the right and had shrouded front forks and enclosed rear suspension springs.

These early exercises really used too much of the road model to be fully effective as trail bikes, but the B105P in particular did point the way and with the arrival of the seventies and a new decade a whole range of Suzuki off-road models appeared.

One of the first was the TC120, called the Trailcat in the USA, and which was derived from the older B105P. In the process it had been the

Early off-road Suzuki, the 80 cc K11T with interesting background of road and racing machines

KT120 for a short while and in these earlier forms retained the wheel diameter of the road model. It used the same engine as before with the oil pump drive off the right end of the crankshaft and flywheel magneto ignition. The gearbox was the dual range 3-speed one with footchange and range lever on the left while both clutch and its lift mechanism went on the right.

The frame was of tubular construction in a spine form. Twin tubes ran back from the headstock along the line of the tank and seat base to the tops of the rear units and then on to form a rear mudguard loop. A second pair of tubes went between the same two points but were formed to drop down to a level above the gearbox before turning up again. Plates welded to their lowest point served to support engine and pivoted fork with the battery and air cleaner above betweeen the two pairs of tube runs. At the front two light tubes ran down from headstock to crankcase shield to take the engine weight.

Telescopic forks went on the front and both wheels had small drum brakes in full width hubs held by wire spokes. The front forks were fitted with a forward facing grab handle to help the rider or others drag it out of any awkward predicament and narrow sports mudguards went around both wheels. The headlight was well

The two sides of the KT120 built 1967–68. It was derived from the B105P and thus based on the B100

tucked in and high, braced bars fitted while the exhaust was raised on the right and came with a heat shield. No centre stand was supplied but lugs for one were and it could be bought as an option. A sturdy prop stand came with the machine and coped with everything except soft mud so few owners had any real problem.

An offshoot to the TC120 appeared around the same time, this being the Alta-Suzuki trials model which was designed by Keith Taylor and built in Wales at Clydach near Swansea. The machine used the TC120 engine unit and wheels in a special frame fitted with REH telescopic forks and new tank, seat, mudguards and ancillaries. It was sold in kit form, which saved the customer the purchase tax then levied on complete machines, was designed specifically as a trials machine and so dispensed with lights. Rather sadly it did not remain on the market for long before rising costs and the appearance of VAT priced it out of contention.

There were several more new models in the Suzuki off-road range at that time and the smallest were the TC90 and TS90, a pair of disc valve engined machines nearly identical in specification except for the gearbox and the rear tyre section. The TS90 had a normal form of gearbox with five speeds in it but the TC90 featured a dual range, as on the TC120, but with four speeds in each range to make eight in all. It also had the fatter rear tyre.

The engines were identical and based on a near vertical single cylinder with the disc valve on the right and flywheel magneto on the left. The engine unit split line was vertical and ran through the cylinder centre while internal construction was conventional. Bore and stroke were 47 × 51·8 mm which gave a capacity of 89·9 cc, compression ratio was 6·8:1 and the power produced was 11 bhp at 7500 rpm. The final drive sprockets differed but the internal box ratios compensated for this and the resulting overall figures for both machines were virtually the same.

The TS90 trail model built 1970–72 with raised exhaust but close fitting front mudguard

Off-road singles

53

The 1971 TC90 with dual range, 4-speed gearbox. The ranges are selected by lever on crankcase top

The frame was tubular with duplex down tubes and a sump plate, front forks telescopic and rear suspension by pivoted fork. Drum brakes and full width hubs were specified and the front mudguard was both short and well clear of the tyre. The exhaust ran to the left and high up just below the seat base and the oil tank for engine lubrication went on the right. A short, skimpy chainguard was fitted and there were no gaiters on the front forks or spring covers on the rear units. A drum shaped air cleaner went behind the cylinder and connected to the carburettor by hose and trunking cast into the crankcase and side cover.

The rider had a dualseat and the machine came with pillion footrests mounted on the rear fork arms but the seat and riding position was cramped for one so carrying a passenger was really reserved for emergencies. A rear carrier was supplied with the TC90 only but both models were fitted with mirrors.

The final off-road model to make its debut just before the seventies was the TS250. This followed the same format as the 90 cc models but with piston controlled induction and engine dimensions of 70 × 64 mm and a capacity of 246 cc. Compression ratio was 6·62:1 and the engine produced 23 bhp at 6500 rpm which went via a 5-speed gearbox to the rear wheel. Most other aspects were as expected with pump

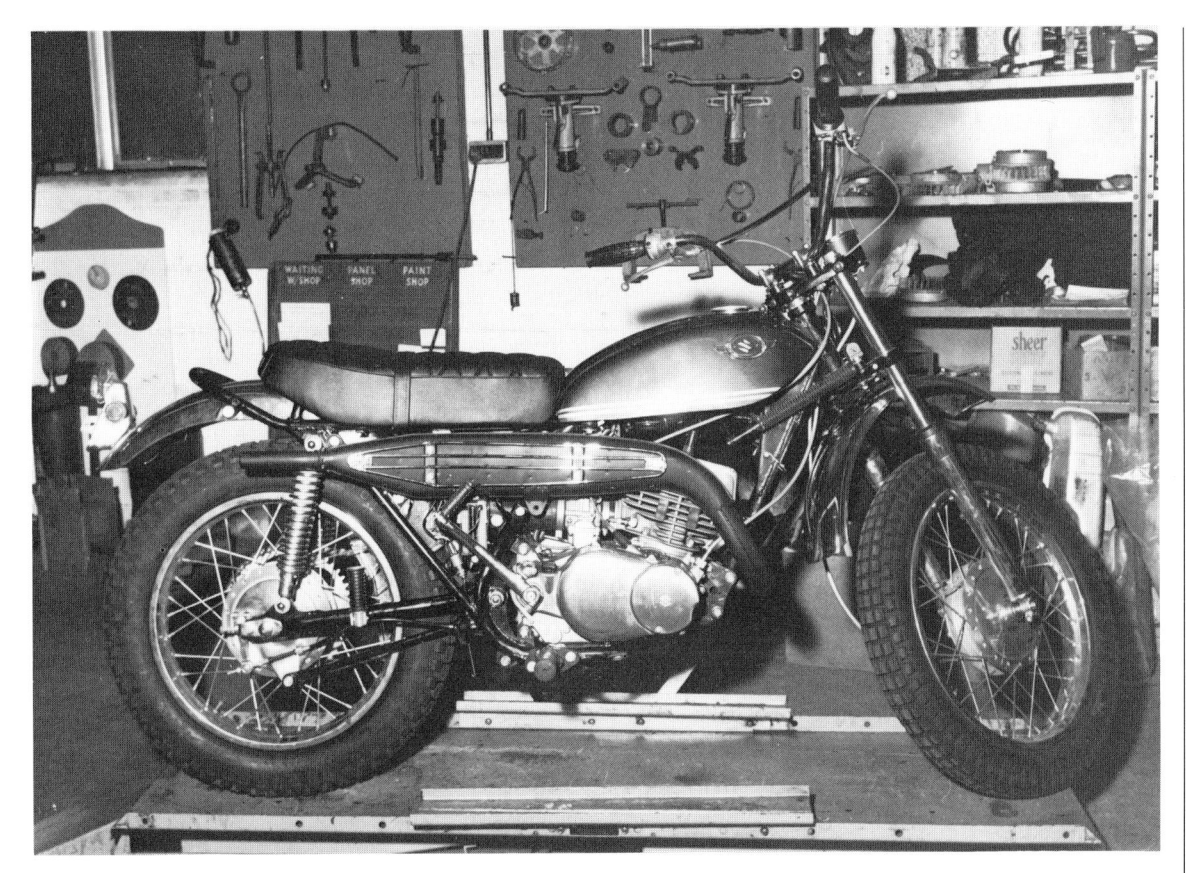

A 1970 TS250, also called the Savage, on a hydraulic bench lift. Useful steering damper fitted

lubrication, flywheel magneto, direct main lighting, small battery to power the stop light and horn and itself charged from the alternator with a rectifier to convert the output to direct current.

The frame was tubular and most items as on the 90s but generally to a larger dimension. One variation was that the exhaust ran high on the right so the oil tank went on the left below the seat although the pump remained at the right end of the crankshaft. The oil continued to be pumped via the mains into the big end but a further feed was taken into the inlet tract to lubricate the back of the piston.

It was to prove to be one of the firm's most popular trail machines and to have a very long life well into the 1980s.

Within a year it had been joined by three more in the series of 50, 125 and 185 cc. The smallest, the TS50, was called the Gaucho in the USA and used the disc valve A50 engine with 5-speed gearbox, set in a spine type tubular frame fitted with telescopic front forks. It was a fully equipped motorcycle that came complete with lights and instruments but in the trail format. Thus the tyres were the universal type, the front mudguard short and the taillight held well clear of the wheel. The exhaust was black and ran low down under the engine before sloping up on the right to bring the outlet up to number plate level. For all its small capacity it worked well and could

55

The TS250 in its 1976 form. Nice style and fully equipped for on- or off-road use

do all manner of short haul runs whether on the road or up the trail.

The second machine was the TS125 and this was fitted with a piston ported engine with 56 × 50 mm dimensions to give 123 cc capacity. Compression ratio was 6·7:1 and power 13 bhp at 7000 rpm. The caruburettor went behind the cylinder and the exhaust pipe, finished in black, ran down under the engine unit with the silencer running up on the right from footrest to seat base. It was protected by a guard plate beneath it and had a heat shield attached to the silencer side.

Lubrication was by pump, ignition by flywheel magneto and the transmission the usual gear primary, wet clutch, 5-speed gearbox and chain on the left under a tiny guard. The unit went into a tubular frame fitted with telescopics and pivoted rear fork and the general fitments were as on the 250.

The third model, the TS185 was modelled on the lines of the 250 with a very similar engine. Dimensions were 64 × 57 mm, capacity 183 cc, compression ratio 6·2:1 and power 17·5 bhp at 7000 rpm. The general construction was very much as the larger machine but there were minor differences in rear tyre and petrol tank size.

The final machine to appear with the various TS models was a mini fun bike made for all terrains. It was the MT50 and used the engine unit from the step-thru model restricted to an putput of 3 bhp at 6000 rpm. The reed valve and side mounted carburettor were retained and the

Left **The Gaucho or TS50, smallest of the trail Suzuki models but still fully fitted out**

Below left **The TS125 Duster model with close front mudguard and rear rack**

Below **TC125. No rack, good mudguard clearance, dual range gearbox and called Prospector**

Off-road singles

transmission continued with the automatic clutch and 3-speed gearbox. Pump lubrication and a flywheel magneto looked after oil and sparks and the cylinder was laid down near to the horizontal.

The frame was a pressed steel spine with telescopics at the front and a short pivoted fork at the rear. Small diameter pressed steel wheels were used and the rims were split into two halves bolted together to enable the 3·50 × 8 in. tyres to be fitted. Both tyres had chunky treads and their mudguards were abbreviated, especially at the front. Small hub brakes went into each wheel and both front and rear were cable operated by hand, the rear lever taking the place of the normal clutch.

A cover went over the top of the frame and also enclosed the fuel tank while the oil tank went on the right. It shape was matched on the left by a cover which concealed the exhaust system and this ran up over the engine and then back. The seat was formed as a dual one, although the machine was only designed to carry the rider, and supported by a single central pillar as a bicycle. Lights and instruments were fitted and the whole machine was small enough to be easily carried in a car for use as a tender on site. Such machines were popular, especially in the USA where it was known as the Trailhopper, on camping and fishing trips as a useful means of picking up shopping or moving about an area from a base camp.

All these models were followed by others as the off-road scene became more popular. For trial riders the TS125 was joined by the TC125 which, as with the two 90s, was the same model fitted with the dual range 4-speed gearbox and a rear carrier. The position of the front mudguard

57

also varied and in time settled into a pattern for all the T series. This gave all the TC machines a sprung guard well clear of the front tyre and their equivalent TS models a close fitting unsprung one. Where only a TS machine was built, as with the 250, it had a sprung guard.

For riders who felt they needed more power Suzuki introduced the TS400. This was on the same lines as the other models but with a bigger engine and some constructional differences. The bore and stroke were 82 × 75 mm giving a capacity of 396 cc, compression ratio was 6·8:1 and power developed 33 bhp at 6000 rpm. A 32 mm Mikuni carburettor tucked in behind the cylinder to feed the piston controlled inlet port and the exhaust ran as on the 125, low down beneath the engine, protected by a sump plate, before

The Apache, otherwise the TS400 for those who like an exciting off-road life

rising at an angle on the right to a tailpipe. The exhaust system was finished in black and had a bright finished heat shield bolted to the silencer.

The ignition system was capacitor discharge and Suzuki gave theirs the name of Pointless Electronic Ignition, or PEI, without perhaps realizing the pitfalls of using the first word. Its double meaning raised a few smiles in the English press when first seen but the firm persevered with it and it became accepted. The operation of the system was as others of the type with a rotating magnet on the crankshaft generating a charging current and a trigger pulse. The charge went to a capacitor and the trigger fired this into the external ignition coil by switching a thyrister, the electronics being assembled into a single sealed unit.

Even more excitement came from riding the TM400 Cyclone which was not all a motocross machine should be

TM250 brochure material; official colour was Phlolina Yellow, known as the Champion

The TS400 engine was unlike its smaller brethren in one or two details. The crankshaft flywheels were bobweights, not full circle, as this in the small crankcase gave enough primary compression for the normal engine running speed. To help starting a compression release valve was fitted into the barrel above the exhaust port and connected to it.

The rest of the engine was normal Suzuki with needle roller big and small ends, two rings on the piston, ball bearing mains and an oil feed through one into the big end. Head and barrel were in light alloy, the latter with a sleeve, and the crankcase halves split on the vertical centre line. The gearbox was all-indirect and the oil pump continued to live under a small cover behind the output sprocket.

The gearbox was 5-speed and of the same basic design as the other models as was the clutch but the operation of the latter was different. In place of the quick-thread and long pushrod was a rack and pinion arrangement on the right. The pinion was turned by a lever on the end of its shaft and the clutch cable ran down the right side of the barrel to pick up with the lever. The rack was a round item that moved in-and-out in the clutch outer cover and was extended through the clutch pressure plate which it thus lifted via a needle roller thrust race.

The TS400 chassis had the same features as the other models with a single frame down-tube joined to duplex tubes that ran beneath the engine unit and then up behind it to a top tube. Suspension was by hydraulically damped units at the rear controlling a pivoted fork and telescopics at the front. Both wheels had wire spokes and drum brakes in full width light alloy hubs. The front mudguard was sprung and well clear of the universal tyre.

The lighting was 12 volt, unlike the other models, and the machine was fully equipped with headlamp, turn indicators, tail and stoplamp, horn, speedometer, rev-counter and mirrors. A hefty kickstart pedal went on the right to commence the action and once underway folded neatly in behind the engine rather better than any of the others.

The trail 400 was preceded by a production motocross model, the TM400, and this was not one of Suzuki's best models. The factory was at the start of a period of great success in the motocross world championships but buyers of the TM400 soon found that it bore little resemblance to the works models. They were smaller, at 370 cc, used petroil mix rather than the oil pump retained on the TM and handled well unlike the TM which did not. A combination of 40 bhp with a frame that flexed meant that even good riders found the machines too tiring to hold while the lesser lights quickly realized they would be faster, safer and happier with a smaller model.

The machine itself was much as the TS400 but on a higher compression ratio of 7·3:1 pushed out its greater power at 6500 rpm. It followed the same lines for engine, transmission and chassis, even to the low slung exhaust system, but with shorter mudguards, competition plates and no road gear.

A year later, in 1972, Suzuki produced a smaller version, the TM250, which sold as the Champion. The 400's name was Cyclone,

The TM125 Challenger from 1973–75. Extra box on end of exhaust to be noted

perhaps an unfortunate choice. The 250 followed the lines of the 400 and was based on the TS250 with a raised compression ratio and other changes to push the power up to 30 bhp at 7500 rpm.

The 250 was followed by the TM125 in 1973 and this used a new engine design with some of the 400 features. Engine dimensions were 56 × 50 mm so the capacity was 123 cc while compression ratio was 7·5:1 and power 20 bhp at 10,000 rpm with a reduction to 18 bhp if a silencer was fitted. Construction was conventional with piston controlled inlet, two large transfer ports, two keystone piston rings, full flywheels and all needle and ball bearing lower half.

Primary drive was by helical gears to a multi-plate wet clutch which was operated by a rack and pinion mechanism as on the 400. The clutch plates were clamped together by seven tension springs which were screwed into tapped holes in the clutch hub and whose outer loops located on cross pins which sat into slot recesses pressed into the pressure plate. A system used quite often by Suzuki over the years.

The gearbox was the usual 5-speed, all-indirect, cross-over drive type with the output sprocket on the left and an added gear pair on the right. The latter meshed with the kickstart and oil pump shaft at the rear and coupled to the clutch drum at the front to give primary starting and to keep the pump turning all the while the engine ran. The pump went into its usual housing behind the sprocket and was linked by cable to the throttle movement.

The ignition system on the 125 was the Suzuki PEI and the expansion chamber low slung beneath the engine and up on the right. The chassis was as for the other models but the wheels had alloy rims and smaller brakes.

The TM range was joined by a 75 in 1973 and a 100 cc model in 1974 while the 400 tried a revised frame but the whole range had gone a little astray. Although the machines were sold as motocross models they lacked feedback from the very successful factory bikes which had won several world championships by then and were what customers expected for their money. In place of a true motocross machine, hopefully firmly based on the previous years works model, they found they had a machine built more for open range racers for the USA market. So the word went round that the TM was more a TS minus lights or even an enduro model but no motocrosser

Right **The Beamish RL250S Mark 2 for 1977 with special frame, forks and many details**

Below right **The Trailhopper or MT50 mini fun bike with the step-thru engine, chunky tyres and strange looks**

Below **Graham Beamish and the RL250 in 1974 outside his Brighton shop**

Suzuki caught their mistake for 1976 after an interim year when they built a few works replica RH250 and RN400 machines. These worked well enough while the factory pushed the new models forward and dealers unloaded their TM bikes. 1976 brought the first of the RM series and these were very successful indeed in sizes that ran from a baby 50 cc to 370 then 400 then 465 and finally 500 cc. Over the years weight dropped, suspension travel increased, full floater rear suspension came and finally water cooling.

Along with the RM in the late 1970s came the

PE enduro models, virtual motocross machines with lights, the DS for desert racing and closer to the trail bikes and a variant typed the RS. Except for the motocross model the size came down to 250 cc for a bigger 4-stroke was also on offer and with this in the range Suzuki motored off-road into the eighties.

The firm was also active in the feet-up or trials area in the early seventies and with this again went rather astray for a while. In 1971 they ran a works machine in England, ridden by Gordon Farley, but this exercise was of limited success as the factory did not follow up the development suggestions the rider put forward.

The machine used was based on the TS250 and when it did go into production in 1973 as the RL250 it was soon known that it reflected Suzuki's keen interest in the USA market rather than the needs of the typical UK trials rider. The machine was quite nice but showed its trail bike origins with a peaky power output and other short-comings.

The RL250 used the TS250 engine unit with the same compression ratio but reduced power output at 18 bhp at 6000 rpm. The 5-speed gearbox was retained but with wider internal ratios and both primary and final drives gave a greater reduction. Ignition was by PEI but lubrication was petroil mix which dispensed with the pump and, usefully, primary kickstart was provided.

The exhaust was up as on the TS but unlike that model the pipe turned straight up from the port and ran over the head and back under the seat and inside the rear subframe on the right of the rear wheel. An expansion box form acted as the main silencer and a further tail unit went at the end.

The chassis was conventional but useful details included offset axle forks and over 11 in. of ground clearance. Less helpful was a short close fitting front mudguard which was no help in muddy conditions. The machine was generally well tucked in with a prop stand laying along the right leg of the rear fork and a narrow, light alloy fuel tank. The seat was short and slim while the air cleaner went up under it and connected to the carburettor by rubber hose. The filter element itself was flat and slid out to the left for servicing.

Useful items were a chain tensioner and an oil drip feed onto the rear chain with the supply kept in the left rear fork leg. Alloy rims and plastic mudguards helped to keep the weight down to 199 lb and the small drum brakes help this. Minor details included cletted footrests and the kick-start lever was specially cranked to clear them.

In the USA the machine carried the name Exacta and worked fairly well. It was prone to lifting its front wheel rather too readily which made hills awkward but pulled well despite the rather peaky power. Unfortunately for Suzuki the expected boom in trials bike sales in the USA failed to appear for the customers preferred the excitements of faster competition or the pleasure of riding their own trail bikes.

The outcome was unusual for a Japanese company. They offered some of the surplus to Beamish Motors who handled the moto-cross Suzuki range in the UK from premises in Brighton on the south coast. Graham Beamish was a very experienced rider and quickly he and his team turned a batch of 50 machines into something more suited to trials work in the UK.

Front mudguard clearance increased, compression ratio went down and flywheel weight went up. The carburettor was restricted and the result was a much improved machine that sold.

Beamish then bought the rest of the RL250 machines that Suzuki were stuck with and really went to work on them. The frame was changed for one developed by Mich Whitlock and during 1975 the machines sold well. So successful was this operation that Suzuki gave Beamish the rights to build their trials models which was an unheard of step for them to take. It proved to be a successful one.

A Mark 2 version came with many detail improvements and was also offered as a trials

Brochure picture of the RV90 Rover all terrain model with its very fat tyres and optional engine guard

sidecar outfit. The major parts of the machine, engine unit, forks and wheels still came from Japan but the frame was English as were quite a number of the detail fittings. This set the pattern for a year or two with each season seeing some useful improvements in the machine while the engine unit remained essentially unchanged.

In 1979 it had a new barrel with reed valve which improved the low down torque and was joined by the slightly larger RL325 whose 322 cc came from enlarging the bore to 80 mm while retaining the 64 mm stroke. Compression ratio was 7·5:1 and power up to 24 bhp at 6500 rpm but in other respects it copied the 250 with PEI, petroil mix lubrication and 5-speed gearbox.

The two models along with a pair of sidecar outfits ran on into the 1980s and went on being successful. The frames continued to come from Whitlock and he also built the sidecar chassis

The smallest all terrain machine, the RV50 which took over from the MT50 in 1973

with its sprung wheel. The brief body was alloy panelled while the fuel tanks continued in the same material. With this and other measures the weight of the 250 solo came down to 188 lb while the 325 was not much more at 201 lb. All told it was a curious but successful arrangement for Suzuki, Beamish and the machine.

Back in 1971 Suzuki had begun to introduce another form of off-road machine in the RV series. These came first in 90 cc form followed by a 50 and 125 in 1973, and were characterized by their small diameter, very fat tyres, raised exhaust and general outline. They were designed as all terrain machines equally at home on road, mud, sand, dirt or snow and in later years were to be superceded by other makes with three wheels.

The engines of the RV50 and RV90 had their single cylinders laid nearly flat to the ground and the heads and barrels were in light alloy with the latter sleeved. Both had reed valve induction into the right side of the crankcase so the carburettor was also on that side as if they were disc valve motors. The exhausts curled up and ran back at high level to silencer, with heat shield, and tail pipe, the 50 one on the left and the 90 on the right. In both cases the tubular air cleaner housing went on the right, above the engine, running back along the frame and connected by hose

The RV125 model on the move. Five gears and rev-counter among the full equipment

and internal crankcase passage to the carburettor.

Lubrication was by pump, ignition by flywheel magneto and primary kick starting was provided so the machines had all the trail or off-road bike virtues. The transmission of each was conventional with clutch and 4-speed gearbox driving a chain on the left to the rear wheel.

The chassis specification read as any other but its form was very different. Fat tyres set the telescopic fork legs well apart and the frame was of the spine design modified to suit the format. The main top beam ran straight back from the headstock to the rear units and, on the 50, into a rear mudguard. From its centre the pressing extended down to support the engine and mount the pivoted rear fork.

The resulting appearance was very different from a normal motorcycle whether on- or off-road for the machine was low but chubby with the solid looking rear half connected by a narrow spine to the front with its fat tyre and resultant wide mudguard. The only earlier model on anything like similar lines had been the MT50 which was dropped once the RV series was established.

The wheels had pressed steel, split rims to aid tyre fitting and the diameter on both models was 10 in. with a 5·40 in. tyre for the RV50 and a 6·70 in. one for the RV90. Single leading shoe drum brakes were used front and rear with normal hand and foot operations for the controls which were completely as usual as the machines came with lights, turn indicators, speedometer and mirrors.

The RV125 was made in a similar form but to a larger set of dimensions. It used a detuned version of the TS125 engine with its 5-speed gearbox. Power was reduced to 10 bhp at 6000 rpm by lowering the compression ratio to 6·3:1 and by fitting a smaller carburettor. The exhaust was in the RV style and on the right side high up with its heat shield.

A cradle frame was used with more substantial forks but without gaiters. The wheels were similar but of different sizes with a 5·40 × 14 in. tyre on the front and a 6·70 × 12 in. on the rear. As on the 90 the dualseat was of a good length with a grab handle behind it and braced handlebars were fitted. The remainder of the equipment was

The RV75 was much as the smaller 50 cc model with four speeds and the same lines

as on the two smaller models except that the 125 came with a rev-counter mounted alongside the speedometer.

The RV series were sold as fun bikes with the 125 listed as the Tracker and the 90 as the Rover in the USA. The series was joined by the RV75 in 1974 and the RV90 Farm bike two years later to give two more models. The first was like the 50 down to its colour and tyres but fitted with the 72 cc engine with 4-speed gearbox while both models could come with a chrome luggage rack bolted on behind the seat.

The basic RV90 was altered that year with forks from the 125 and both models had already adopted close fitting unsprung mudguards the year before in place of the original sprung type. The Farm Bike was a variant aimed at the Australian outback with its vast areas and special needs. The machine was simply better protected and fitted out for carrying goods and surviving a minor spill far from base. Thus the seat was shortened and a very large rear carrier added while a tubular guard ran down from the headstock to under the engine with a sump plate welded to it. This guard was also offered for the stock RV90 as an option.

The concept of the RV series was interesting and the machines certainly did their job well but they went from the range in the late seventies for they were superseded by the all terrain vehicle with its three balloon tyres. This went everywhere and was stable, able to carry more and could be built with power take off and many accessories. In many ways it was even more fun so the two-wheel type was replaced overnight.

The RV was short lived but the trail series ran on and on. There were changes of course and an early one was to upgrade the two 90 cc models into the TC100 and TS100 while dropping the original TC120 Trailcat around the same time. The extra capacity of the 100 models came from boring the cylinders out to 49 mm wich with the 51·8 mm stroke gave a capacity of 97·7 cc. The compression ratio dropped to 6·5:1 and the

Above **The TC185 with 5-speed, dual range gearbox, sprung mudguard and rear rack**

Top **The 1976 TS75 with very minimal front mudguard and convoluted exhaust system**

power remained at 11 bhp but at a lower engine speed of 7000 rpm.

Otherwise the machines continued as before with disc valve engine and 4-speed, dual range gearbox for the TC, and plain 5-speed for the TS. The exhausts were altered to copy the 125 so they ran under the engine and sloped up on the right with a heat shield on the silencer and a sump guard under the pipe. The TC continued the style in mudguards by having the front sprung while the TS one was close fitting. The TC also had a luggage grid fitted behind its dualseat. Both models had braced handlebars and full road equipment but no rev-counters. Only the TS100 had turn indicators but the TC100 had the mounting stalks at the front and fitting holes at the rear.

The larger TS185, TS250 and TS400 had all changed their ignition systems to PEI by 1972, the last year of the 90s, and in 1974 they and the two 125s were fitted with 21 in. front tyres. The same year also saw the introduction of two more trail models, one in a new capacity.

This was the TS75 which was similar to the TM75 and had a near horizontal engine with 4-speed gearbox in cycle parts much as the TS50. The second machine was the TC185 which duplicated the TS185 except for the gearbox which was a dual range 5-speed unit giving the rider a choice of ten ratios. Unlike the TS version it used a 19 in. front wheel but with sprung mudguard mounted well clear of the tyre. As with other TC models it was fitted with a rear luggage rack but unlike all the other trail bikes the TC185 had coil ignition and an electric starter, obtained by using the dynamo and special wiring.

1976 brought a Farm Bike version of the TC100 with a bigger rear rack than standard and crash guards round the front of the exhaust system and the ends of the handlebars. The latter protected the clutch and brake levers in the event of a spill. A longer front mudguard with mud flap was fitted and a shorter seat but otherwise the machine was as the standard model.

At the end of that year all the TC models were dropped from the range together with the two extremes from the TS series, the 50 and the 400. There was no longer any real call for dual range gearboxes and the very small and very large models were in one case too cramped and slow while in the other really too fast for comfort. On the trail a 250 cc 2-stroke was adequate for most while for those seeking more grunt they introduced the SP series with single cylinder 4-stroke engines.

The TS75 only lasted another year before it too went, leaving four TS models in 100, 125, 185 and 250 cc capacities. These ran on into the eighties but in new forms from around 1978. The smallest, the TS100 lost its disc valve and in its new form had a reed valve in the induction passage as did the other three models. One, the TS125, was fitted with a 6-speed gearbox but all the others continued with five. The styling changed and became more uniform with all exhausts turned up to run high along on the right just below tank and seat. The larger pair had sprung front mudguards, the smaller ones being unsprung and close fitting. All four engines looked very similar.

So Suzuki ran on with its 2-strokes off-road on trail, enduro or motocross with an up-to-the-minute range that reflected modern technology just as the first K11T had done.

4 Little twins, big twins

Suzuki twins date back to 1956 when their first 250 was built as the Colleda TT model. It was soon followed by the TP and then, in 1960, by the Twinace models, the TA and TB. With these 250s came the smaller Colleda Seltwin machines of 125 and 150 cc capacity and these served the firm well up to the early 1960s. By then the styling had become lighter and much improved while the company was learning a good deal about the 2-stroke engine and its possibilities. With this knowledge they were well placed to continue their twins in the three sizes to complement their range of singles.

The two smaller twins were the S30 and S32 which shared many parts in both engine and chassis and were complemented by the S31 with sports styling. The largest twin was the T10 and this was clearly based on the older Twinace model.

The smallest machine was the S30 with engine dimensions of 42 × 45 mm giving it a capacity of 124·7 cc. The compression ratio was 7·0:1 and on this it produced 11 bhp at 7000 rpm, breathing through a single carburettor. The S31 used the same engine but fitted with twin carburettors which enabled it to give 12 bhp at 8000 rpm. The slightly larger S32 produced the same power but at 7000 rpm and was in effect the same engine just bored out to 46 mm and 149·6 cc capacity. Compression ratio was a little higher at 7·4:1 and it too had twin carburettors. All three models had two separate exhausts, one on each side, with

TWO EXAMPLES OF *SUZUKI'S* TECHNOLOGICAL CAPABILITY.

TRY THE SUZUKI 250 TB.. THE SPORTS CYCLE WITH A DYNAMO STARTER!

For quick starting, high riding and smart styling, the 250 TB is the motorcycle for the true sportsman.
Check these performance figures:
- Starting System....Dynamo Starter
- Maximum Speed....85 m.p.h.
- Maximum Power....18 HP/7,000 r.p.m.
- Fuel Consumption....127 mile/Imp. gallon
- Climbing Ability (low gear)....1/3
- Brake Front....Internal expanding type hand brake
- Rear....Internal expanding type oil brake operated by foot

FOR JET-AGE LINES AND LIGHTWEIGHT DESIGN RIDE THE 125 SG......

Featuring a twin-cylinder, dual carburetor engine design, the 125 SG is unexcelled in economical fuel consumption and efficient performance.

Performance Figures:
- Starting System....Dynamo Starter
- Maximum Speed....65.2 m.p.h.
- Maximum Power....11.0 HP/7,000 r.p.m.
- Fuel consumption....142 mile/Imp. gallon
- Climbing Ability (low gear)....1/3

SUZUKI 250TB   SUZUKI 125SG

SUZUKI MOTOR CO., LTD.

HEAD OFFICE: TAKATSUKA, NEAR HAMAMATSU-CITY, JAPAN
TOKYO BRANCH: 1, 5-CHOME, SHIBA-SHINBASHI, MINATOKU, TOKYO, JAPAN

Left **An early twin advert taken from** Motor Cycling **in 1961. The 125 styling is earlier than the 250**

Above **The T10 in 1963 when the 250 twin related to the earlier Colleda models**

those of the S30 and S32 running back low down to very lengthy silencers. The S31 wore its pipes raised to run at crankcase top level but still with long silencers, albeit fitted with a heat shield on each side.

The cylinders were inclined forward a little and the plugs laid back in the light alloy cylinder heads so they remained vertical. Piston controlled induction was used so the carburettors went behind the barrels where they connected by hose to an air cleaner.

The general construction of the engine followed conventional lines for the time with the gearbox built in unit with it. The primary drive went on the right and, as the gearbox was of the all-indirect, cross-over type, the fully enclosed rear chain was on the left. The clutch was a wet multi-plate type and the gearbox contained four speeds. Two forms of gearchange were offered, the standard being the return type with N, 1, 2, 3, 4 sequence so that neutral was a full pedal movement past first. There was also the option of a rotary shift which gave the facility of changing from top to neutral with the return sequence in a continuous loop in either direction.

Lubrication was by petroil mix with the initial ratio of 15:1 reducing to a slightly lower pollution producing 20:1 once the engine was run in. Igni-

Suzuki Two-strokes

74

tion was by a pair of coils with twin contact breakers opened by a single lobe cam on the left end of the crankshaft. Inboard of the cam went a combined dynamo and starter unit which performed both functions by switching the wiring as necessary. The electric system was 12 volts.

To back up the electric starter a kickstart mechanism was fitted into the gearbox behind the output shaft. This terminated in a shaft protruding from the primary drive cover but the kickstart lever was not normally fitted to it. Instead it was capped and the lever carried separately as an emergency aid.

The frame was the spine type, built up from steel pressings, with a support tube bolted between the headstock and the front of the crankcase. Telescopic front forks were fitted and had exposed springs on the sporting S31 but these were gaitered on the other two models. At the rear went a pivoted fork and again the springs were enclosed on the tourers and exposed on the sports model.

Wheels were built up with steel rims, wire spokes and full-width, light alloy hubs each of which contained a single leading shoe drum brake. The front mudguard on all three models was narrow and supported by a single cross-stay on each side while the rear one was formed as an extension of the main frame. The S31 alone had a mud flap fitted to the tail of its front mudguard. Tyres on the 125 cc models were 3·00 × 16 in. while for the 150 they were 2·75 × 17 in.

Claimed performance was 62 mph for the S30 and 68 mph for the other two models which was recorded on the speedometer set in the top of the headlamp shell. The instrument carried two warning lights with neutral on the right and a charge lamp on the left. Ahead of the speedometer and to the left went the ignition switch and this had four positions for off, ignition, lights

The Suzuki stand at Earls Court in 1966 with Alan Kimber, the man then in charge, chatting the ladies

and park. The left handlebar carried the horn button and dipswitch while the right had the same horizontally moving control for turn indicators and a button for the electric starter. The controls were normal with the carburettor cold start lever mounted on the units left on the models with twin instruments. On the early, single carburettor S30 the lever went in the centre of the handlebars.

The T10 followed the same lines of construction as the smaller twins but was based on engine dimensions of 52 × 58 mm which gave it a capacity of 246 cc. The actual compression ratio was 6·3:1 and on this the engine developed 21 bhp at 8000 rpm.

The cylinders were inclined forward a little and the plugs lay back so were near to being upright. Each cylinder head was separately cast in light alloy with 11 vertical fins and held down by four bolts threaded into the barrel. Its combustion chamber was part spherical, without squish band, and a copper and asbestos gasket went between head and barrel, the latter cast in iron.

The barrels were separate and each held down

Below **The Suzuki Super Six T20 in 1966 with rear carrier added. Six speeds and twin leading shoes**

Right **Tommy Robb on the T20 at Brands Hatch in the 1966 500 mile race**

Little twins, big twins

Above **The super sports twin, the T21 in 1966 with more power and same chassis as T20**

Below **For trail riding the TC250 used the T21 engine and raised exhausts**

by nuts onto four small studs screwed into the crankcase top. The porting was conventional in layout with transfers and single exhaust. This was an oval port which led to a round exit where a face was machined into which went three studs to take the exhaust pipe flange. The inlet port was bridged and ran back to a stub to which the carburettor was clamped.

Each piston had a domed crown and carried two rings, the top one chrome plated and the second parkerized. The gudgeon pin hole was offset forward by 1·5 mm and each side was cut away to match the transfer ports. The ring groove pins were in phosphor-bronze and the gudgeon pins were circlip retained.

The crankshaft was pressed together with one central and two outer ball bearing mains, oil seals, and roller big ends. The flywheels were small and full circles with the inner sides relieved to accommodate the connecting rod end but otherwise spaced just to clear the rod. They were a close fit in their crankcase chambers.

The crankshaft carried a starter-cum-dynamo on its left end with two sets of contact points mounted on the outer surface of the stator assembly. On the end of the crankshaft went a centrifugal advance mechanism and this moved a single lobe cam which opened the points in turn every 180 degrees of crankshaft rotation. Battery powered coil ignition was used.

Lubrication was by petroil mix with an initial ratio of 15:1 reducing to 20:1 once the engine

T200 controls with combined instruments and vertically set distance recorder

was run in. The mixture was supplied by a pair of 20 mm slide type carburettors with integral float chambers and butterfly chokes. The two instruments were handed to suit the chokes and access to the ticklers, throttle screws, pilot screws and fuel lines.

The gearbox was built in unit with the engine and the crankcase which contained both assemblies was split on its horizontal centre line through the centre of the crankshaft, both gearbox shafts and the kickstarter. The cases were die-cast in light alloy and had cooling fins incorporated. Maintenance was assisted by the handbook listing the diameter and length of each of the 15 bolts which held the case halves together and the case carrying the order in which they were to be tightened. In the bearing journals in the case halves were set pins, or dowels, and circlip grooves to locate the bearings axially and radially.

Primary transmission was by a pair of helical gears to the clutch with five friction and five steel plates clamped up by six tensions springs in the unique Suzuki style. The gearbox was all-indirect, crossover with four speeds and these were selected by forks which slid on the barrel cam which guided their movement. A positive stop mechanism behind the clutch turned the cam and was itself worked by a cross-shaft with the gear pedal on its end on the left. It emerged from the crankcase low down and just aft of the gearbox sprocket.

Above that item went the neutral indicator light switch, operated by the end of the selector cam, and forward of it the clutch pushrod through the centre of the input shaft. The clutch was lifted by a quick thread in the left outer cover which actuated the pushrod and via it the mushroom and pressure plate. The gearbox shafts each ran in one ball bearing and one bush with the latter supporting the more lightly laden end of the shaft.

Side covers enclosed the primary drive and the dynamo plus gearbox sprocket while a small added cover gave access to the contact points. Further covers went over the carburettors to enclose these items. The complete engine and gearbox unit was located by three bolts around the rear of the crankcase plus two which attached to lugs on the rear of the cylinder barrels.

A true spine frame was used with the engine hung from the centre section that also carried the rear pivoted fork. The main frame beam was built up from two pressings welded together with strengthening plates around the engine and rear fork area. The tail of the frame was a separate pressing which bolted into place to form the back half of the rear mudguard.

At the front went telescopic forks of conventional design with enclosed springs acting as the suspension medium and oil providing hydraulic damping and lubrication. The forks turned in ball bearings in the head races and these were adjusted with the usual stem-nut and lock-nut.

1967 T200, much as the 250, but physically a smaller machine all round

A steering damper was fitted and at the rear went spring units with hydraulic damping.

The wheels had steel rims, wire spokes and full width, light alloy hubs containing the drum brakes. That at the front was a single leading shoe device operated by cable from the right handlebar lever but at the rear the hydraulic operation of the Twinace was retained. This introduced a fair amount of complication in an era when hydraulic brakes were virtually unknown in the motorcycle field and few mechanics had any working knowledge of them.

The master cylinder went on the right just behind the rear fork pivot where it was operated by the brake pedal. The hose ran along the fork leg back to the rear hub and connected to the double acting slave cylinder. An external, spring loaded lever acted as means of setting the shoe clearance and the link between pedal and master cylinder could be adjusted to set the desired free play. In all it amounted to a good few parts in place of the usual pedal, rod and cam lever used on other models and it made rear wheel removal more awkward.

As on the S twins the front mudguard was narrow, sporting and held by a single cross-stay on each side. At the front this ran forward of the guard to form a loop ahead of it. The rear mudguard was an extension of the frame so heavily valanced and it carried a flat tail at its end to keep the mud and water well clear of the rider or passenger. Both wheels were shod with 3·00 × 17 in. tyres with a ribbed section at the front and a studded at the rear. Both had whitewall sides.

The fuel tank was rubber mounted and secured by bolts. It had chrome plated sides carrying kneegrips and a substantial look that was belied by its small capacity, mainly lost due to its large tunnel for the frame. A cross tube allowed fuel to flow from one side to the other but meant draining was needed before removal. At the front, on the left, a transparent pipe ran

Interesting T500 clay model, one of several built to determine the line and styling

up the tank to serve as a fuel gauge. The single, 3-position fuel tap went on the left and incorporated a reserve, a strainer and a separate connection for each carburettor.

A dualseat was provided, held by a clip at the front and two nuts at the rear, and the pillion footrests were mounted on the rear fork. Behind the seat went a luggage rack and below it on each side went plated covers, each secured by a single handscrew. On the right the cover enclosed the battery, fuse, regulator and turn indicator relay while on the left went the rear brake reservoir and the toolkit. Included with the tools was a 200 cc tin of brake fluid and the manual indicates that while the system was supplied filled with fluid the tank cap lacked a vent hole. This the dealer was required to drill when preparing the machine for sale.

When parked, the owner had the choice of centre or prop stands, the first sturdy but the second angling the machine rather too far over for use on soft ground.

The instruments and controls were very much as for the smaller twins and the wiring diagrams have much in common including the colour code. Speedometer, warning lights and switches all followed the same pattern but there were minor variances in ignition switch, dynamo regulator and starter relay, the last two items being combined in one for the T10.

Turn indicators were included in the specification and the electric horn hung from the frame above the cylinder heads. The headlamp continued with its inverted horse-shoe shape and reports gave it high marks.

In fact the whole machine was well regarded with a top speed just below 80 mph, good accelerations, good handling and an excellent front brake. The rear brake was not so well liked, being spongy in operation, and was the worst major feature of the machine. The contemporary English reports both suggested that the model had a buzzer which sounded a warning when

Suzuki Two-strokes

the ignition was turned on but in fact this was the turn signal relay vibrating its contact points as it charged its condenser.

The twin range of four models continued with little change for a year or two although the S30 did gain a second carburettor to match the others in the series. Then late in 1965 came a new version of the 250, the T20 which quickly became known as the Super Six.

The T20 was a major step forward for Suzuki and while it was superficially similar to the T10, in truth it was a completely new model with only the barest link with the past. With it Suzuki took a big step into the future and it has to be the fore-runner of their modern twin range. With it came pump lubrication, six gears, a tube frame and super-sports performance.

The new engine was just that—completely new in all respects. Even the basic dimensions altered to an all-square 54 mm which moved the capacity to 247 cc. Both compression ratio and power output were raised, the first to 7·3:1 and the second to 29 bhp at 7500 rpm. New features for the engine unit were pump lubrication, left kickstart and the 6-speed gearbox from which it got its name. About all that remained from the T10 was the constructional conception of

An early American advert for the T500 before it became known as the Titan

Above **1968 T500 in the UK so cast as the Cobra. Exhausts pass outside frame on this model**

Below **A T250 from the period 1969–72. Machine developed from the T20 with similar features**

horizontal crankcase split, inclined cylinders and outer covers for primary drive and generator.

The heads and barrels remained separate but the fixing changed to eight long studs in the crankcase and eight long sleeve nuts to locate the heads and clamp them to the barrels. The plugs continued to lay back a little in the heads which were cast in light alloy while each head gasket became a 0·5 mm thick aluminium plate.

The barrel was new and in light alloy with a cast iron liner shrunk into place. It was flanged for location at the top and the dimensions brought the flange slightly proud of the surrounding alloy to ensure it sealed firmly against the head gasket. The porting was normal but the timing differed from that of the T10 and the port shapes and areas were altered. The port edges were provided with chamfers to ease the life of

Suzuki Two-strokes

84

Left **The 90 cc twin from 1969 with near horizontal cylinders and stylish exhaust**

Far left **The 125 cc Stinger with horizontal barrels; first T125 was as T200 and in different frame**

Below left **The T350 Rebel in 1971, a machine very much as the 250 but quicker**

the piston rings and while small at most points these chamfers extended for 5 mm below the exhaust and 10 mm below each transfer in a half-moon form.

The outer ends of the ports also altered with the exhaust becoming round with an external thread which took a ring nut to secure the exhaust pipe. To ensure these stayed in place each was locked by a clamp held by a screw and these went between the two ports so were readily accessible. On the inlet side the stub was changed to a flange with two studs onto which fitted the carburettor with a heat shield between it and the barrel.

The piston continued with domed crown but the pin offset reduced to 1 mm and was to the rear, not the front. The rings remained two in number but were of keystone section with the top face angled down and in at seven degrees. Both rings were the same and were soft chrome treated to assist running-in. The gudgeon pins were still hollow and retained by circlips.

The bottom half of the engine continued with its pressed-up construction, small-diameter full-circle flywheels and three ball bearing mains. The connecting rods were steel forgings and both big and small ends turned on caged needle rollers. Four oil seals were fitted to the crankshaft, one at each end outboard of the outer main and two in the centre either side of that bearing. The outer mains were lubricated by the oil flowing through them en route to collector discs which supplied the big ends, the fling from them looking after the small ends and pistons. The centre main was supplied with oil from the gearbox which passed through a U tube cavity into the bearing and drained back to the transmission chamber.

The electrical system was new with a rotating magnet alternator fitted on the left end of the crankshaft and connected to a fullwave rectifier. In daytime one pair of coils was in use but all three came into operation when the headlamp was on. The two sets of ignition contact points remained fitted on the outer side of the stator but the timing was fixed so the cam went directly on the end of the crankshaft.

The primary drive remained on the right with a helical gear on the crankshaft turning the clutch drum. This ran on a pair of caged needle roller bearings and contained six friction and seven steel plates, the latter splined to the clutch centre. Six clutch springs clamped the plates together with the pressure plate on the inside of the assembly as the release lever went on the right of the clutch. It worked through a ball bearing thrust race and spring plate to release the clutch and the lever was located in the primary drive cover.

The gearbox was all new with its six speeds but remained of the all-indirect, cross-over type with the output sprocket on the left. Ball races continued to be used in the load areas and the other ends of the shafts were supported by needle races, the same form of bearing also going in the two largest gears, one on each shaft. A needle thrust race on the input shaft took the end loading of the clutch operation.

Gear selection continued to be by forks which worked on a barrel cam but their number was up to three and the whole assembly went in the lower crankcase half below the gearbox shafts unlike the T10 where it was above them. The neutral switch stayed on the left end of the cam and the positive stop mechanism on the right with the pedal shaft running across and out on the left.

A curious feature of the selection mechanism was that it sought to retain features from both

Oil tank, sight window, filter and oil pump of T350. Note rev-counter drive from pump top

old and new styles of Japanese gearbox. Thus the box changed from first to second in one movement but when coming down through the gears went from second to neutral in one move and neutral to first in another. In this way neutral could be positively selected when coming to a halt.

The kickstart shaft was aft of the gearbox output one as usual but extended out to the left so the pedal, a folding one, went on that side. The reason for the change was the appearance of the engine oil pump on the right, bolted to the outside of the primary drive cover, and driven from a gear running on the right end of the kickstart shaft. This meshed with one running free on the output shaft which in turn coupled with one locked to the back of the clutch drum.

Thus, through this train and the primary drive, the oil pump was directly coupled to the crankshaft so driven all the time the engine turned. The same train also gave primary kickstarting without going through the clutch so the engine could be started when in gear as long as the clutch was lifted. The train had one more job to do as the last gear was locked to a skew gear which drove a near vertical shaft set in the outer

cover and this was connected by flexible cable to the rev-counter to register engine speed.

The running parts of the engine were encased in the two crankcase halves plus side covers which in turn had access plates for maintenance. As on the T10, three bolts attached the crankcase to the frame but as with the engine, this was completely new.

Unlike earlier twins the frame of the T20 was on much more traditional lines being constructed from tubes and of the duplex cradle type. Twin tubes ran from the headstock down under the front of the engine and then back and up to the tops of the rear suspension units. Two more tubes ran forward from this point to the down tubes and the headstock was braced with a single tube running from its top back to the upper pair. Cross-tubes kept the two cradles apart and sheet gussets provided bracing and mountings for rear units, pivoted fork and minor details.

Front forks were telescopic with hydraulic damping and they were matched by the rear units. Both front and rear suspension springs were exposed and a steering damper was fitted to the front forks. The rear fork moved on plain bushes.

Both wheels had steel rims, wire spokes and full width, light alloy hubs with drum brakes. Wheel diameter was 18 in. and the tyre sections were 2·75 in. front and 3·00 in. rear. The hydraulic operation of the rear brake was dropped and replaced by a cable for the single leading shoe while at the front went a twin leading shoe assembly. The actuating cable connected to the forward lever and this was linked to the second one by an adjustable rod.

Above right **The 1971 T500R known as the Charger. Fast, reliable but no panache**

Right **Early and odd 1973 GT125 with drum front brake and special tank striping. Ram-air cooling**

Little twins, big twins

Separate mudguards were fitted front and rear with the first still narrow and supported by a single thin cross-stay on each side. The rear mudguard retained a valance which gave it strength so no stays were needed. A dualseat was fitted but the passenger footrests were no longer on the rear fork legs but on extensions from the main frame that also supported the silencers which ran low down on each side, clamped to the exhaust pipes and recessed on the top for the rear wheel spindle.

The fuel tank was as on the T10 with tap on the left and the external level gauge. It retained its chrome plated side panels and the kneegrips, and was joined by an oil tank which fitted below the seat on the right of the machine. The oil tank had a sight bubble set in the outer face low down for level checking and its outlet was fitted with a strainer and a magnet to ensure that no debris reached the oil pump.

The oil tank was matched on the left by a cover and behind this went the tools and the battery, rectifier and fuse. Between the covers and ahead of the centrally located battery went an air filter housing which clipped to both carburettor intakes.

Both centre and prop stands were fitted and controls and instrumentation were similar to the T10 except for the omission of turn indicators. This kept the horn button and dip switch together on the left while the charge warning light was replaced by one for high beam. The neutral light remained and was located in the combined instrument unit which was fitted into the top of the headlamp shell.

The GT250 in 1973 with Ram-air cooling and disc front brake

This incorporated speedometer and rev-counter in one assembly with each needle swinging through half a turn or so from the 12 o'clock position to reach its maximum. The speedometer was on the left and both needles moved in a clockwise direction. A distance recorder was built in as well and was positioned in the arc of the speedometer scale to give its reading as a vertical line of figures.

The Suzuki Super Six was an immediate sensation and the start of a series that was to run on for many years. It was quickly tested by the press and found to be good for over 90 mph with searing acceleration. The gearchange was light and positive, the brakes powerful and the handling precise. There was some vibration but not too much and the riding position and control layout and operation were thought excellent. In terms of performance, detail design and engineering the T20 set new standards that were fully appreciated world wide.

In a few months it was also making its mark on the race circuits and one ran in the 1966 250 cc TT. Preparation was minimal with the engine left standard and most attention given to fitting rear-sets, clip-ons, fairing and bigger fuel tank. It ran without fuss to 12th position using the stock silencers and consuming a gallon of fuel per lap.

Far less well known was the T21 which was a more sporting version of the twin with compression ratio raised to 7·8:1 and the power to 30·5 bhp at 8000 rpm. The cycle parts differed in that the suspension springs were exposed and

A 1973 T500 with unusual engine protection bar built onto crash bar

Little twins, big twins

89

the finish was changed but otherwise it was a repeat of the Super Six.

In 1967 it became the T250 at home in Japan and was joined by the TC250 in street scrambler guise. This model used the same engine but had raised exhausts, gaitered forks and fatter tyres for a little off road use.

Early in 1967 the twins were joined by a further model which was the first of a pair to replace the S series. The new machine was the T200 and very much as the 250. The engine size was smaller with dimensions of 50 × 50 mm and the capacity was 196 cc. Compression ratio was 7·0:1 and power produced 23 bhp at 7500 rpm.

The model, also called the Invader, looked like the T20 but was in fact all new for it was built to a reduced scale in most dimensions. It followed the larger model's design closely and the resemblance was so good that it was only when the two were side by side that the scale reduction was apparent.

There were differences apart from the capacity and overall dimensions for the 200 only had five gears. In other respects it followed the same paths with twin cylinders, pressed up crankshaft, horizontal crankcase split and pump lubrication. One useful change was a move by the transmission filler cap from beneath the air cleaner on the 250 to the primary drive cover where it was far more accessible.

External changes were the fitting of turn indicators, a diaphragm fuel tap connected to the left carburettor stub and one-piece construction for each exhaust pipe and silencer. These were still held to the barrels by ring nuts.

Otherwise it was the T20 and gave the same sparkling performance. Top speed was in excess of 80 mph, acceleration was very brisk indeed and fuel consumption as good as 80 mpg over a test distance although this could drop well below 50 mpg if a high cruising speed was main-

GT125 on show with special tank, seat and side covers to go with drop bars

Little twins, big twins

tained. A street scrambler TC200 was also built and followed the lines of the 250 with raised pipes while retaining most of the stock parts.

1967 also saw the introduction of another twin but this was no S series replacement but a move into a bigger class altogether. The machine was at first listed as the 500/Five and took the name Titan in the USA and Cobra in the UK. In time it was just listed as the T500 and became one of the most underrated models of all time.

It appeared in the pre-dawn of a new age of motorcycling, the era of superbikes, and this is usually heralded as starting with the introduction of the exhilarating Kawasaki Mach III and the svelte Honda CB750. Both these models first appeared late in 1968 and both offered tremendous performance with, in one case, a very exciting ride, or in the other, very comprehensive equipment. Their appearance completely overshadowed the Suzuki which had been about for more than a year but lacked their panache.

In truth the T500 was a very quick machine that time showed to be as reliable as a stone but unable to grab attention. Discerning riders used them for years, delighting in the bullet proof engine and accepting its vibration and thirst. It was the first big 2-stroke to be built for many a long year and completely put to rest the idea that large capacity twins using that form of engine cycle would overheat and seize. The Suzuki did not, even when run by one magazine through the summer heat of Death Valley, California, one of the hottest places in the world and in parts running below sea level.

The problem of the T500 was that it looked too small, too ordinary and too humdrum to catch the market's attention. Customers either went for the raw excitement of the Kawasaki or the sophistication of the big Honda; the Suzuki just looked too staid to deliver the goods. Those who found out the truth about it, loved it but they did not amount to the big crowd the firm hoped for so in time they turned to their big triple to keep their market share.

The machine that was at the heart of this was a simple twin cylinder much on the lines of the other models. While the basic format was the same there were a good number of changes in the design details both in the engine unit and the chassis.

The engine was based on dimensions of 70 × 64 mm, the same as the 250 cc singles were to use, and the resulting capacity was 493 cc. Compression ratio was 6·6:1 and the power output was first given as 46 bhp at 7000 rpm, this rising by one to 47 from 1969 on. The overall format of the engine unit was as the T20 but with quite a number of differences in the details.

Thus the cylinders continued in light alloy with iron sleeves and the heads clamped down onto aluminium gaskets and were held by four sleeve nuts secured to studs in the crankcase top. Different was the addition of four more bolts to hold the head onto the barrel, these being interspersed between the main nuts. All eight were in a symmetrical pattern turned to match the barrels and the porting. This was moved round the cylinder axis to splay the exhausts well out and to give the inner transfers more room.

The outside of the barrel also differed with the exhaust pipe ring secured by two bolts and the pipe a sliding fit into the long, tapered silencer. On the inlet side the flanges remained but had intake hoses bolted to them and the carburettors fitted into these and retained by clips.

The bottom half of the engine was a repeat of the 250 with needle races in the connecting rod ends, three mains, four crankshaft seals and the normal Suzuki oil feed to the big ends. The alternator went on the left with the points outboard of it and the helical gear primary drive on the right. The clutch had seven each of cork lined and steel plates but differed in that it ran on a bronze bush and was released in the more usual way with a quick-thread on the left and a push-rod through the gearbox shaft. Six springs clamped the plates together.

The gearbox followed the usual pattern of all-indirect and cross-over drive but was otherwise totally different and all new. It contained five speeds and unlike other models had all five gears on the input shaft fixed to it while all five on the output ran free and on caged needle races. Four of the races were of the split type and assembled to areas of the shaft that had been ground down to take them. The rest of the shaft was splined

Above **By 1975 the GT250 had lost its fork gaiters and had a new tank lining**

Left **Publicity picture of T500 taken in 1975, still drum brake at front**

Little twins, big twins

93

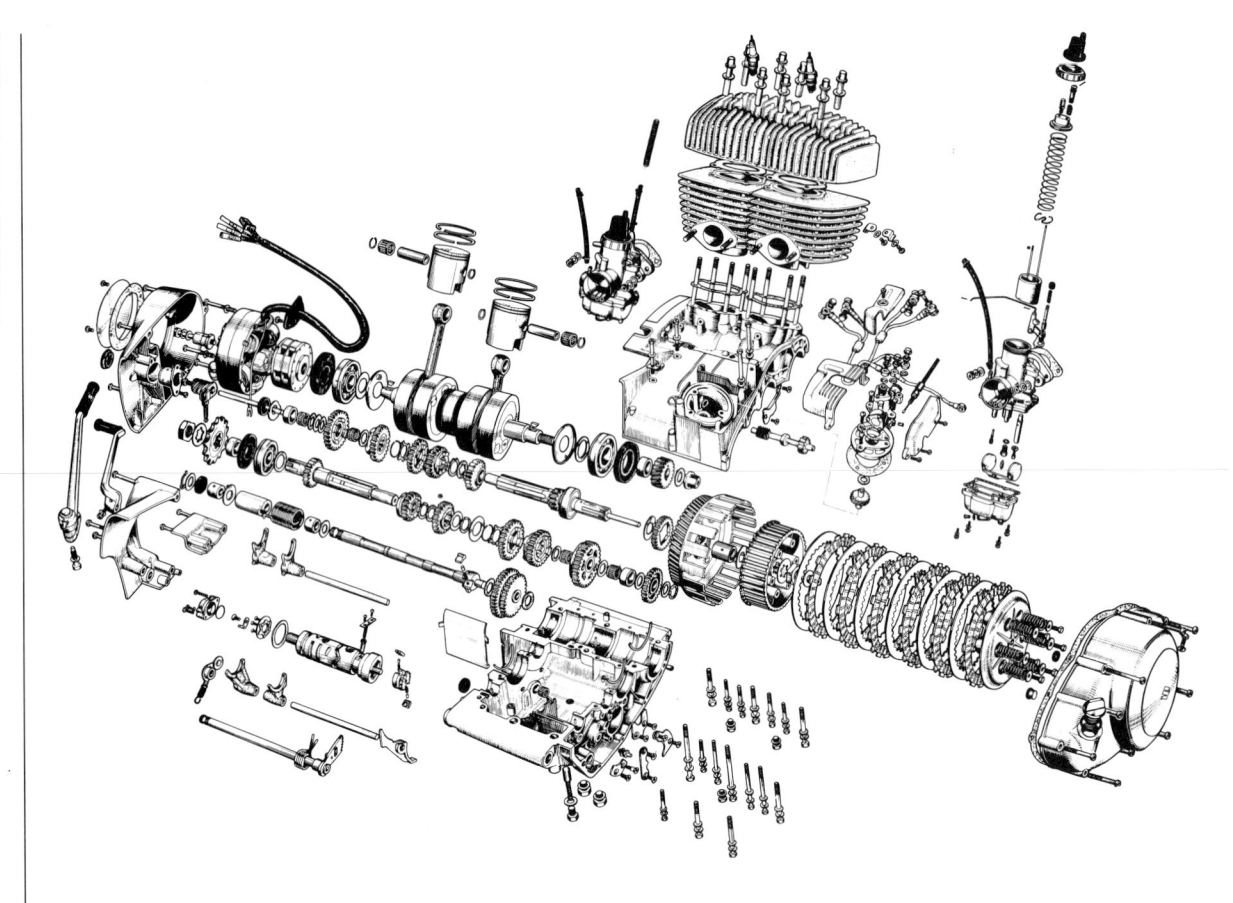

Exploded line drawing of typical twin engine unit, the T250, with oil pump on crankcase top

and carried three selector dogs which moved to and fro to engage the gears.

Their movement was controlled by a trio of selector forks which slid on a single cross shaft and were moved by a barrel cam fitted beneath them. Each fork had an extension pin which ran in one track in the cam. From then on the mechanism was stock Suzuki with positive stop built into the right end of the cam, gear change shaft extended out to the left for the lever and neutral light switch at the left end of the cam.

The kickstart shaft went aft of the gearbox output shaft and the lever was on the left. It worked via the gearbox bottom gear pair to turn the clutch so the box had to be in neutral before the engine was started.

The kickstart gear also drove the oil pump but this was mounted in a new position on top of the upper crankcase in a cast recess above the gearbox. The pump drive was as the rev-counter on the 250 with a skew gear made as one with the kickstart pinion and meshed with a vertical shaft. This drove the oil pump, which was no different in design to others used by Suzuki, and the dirve was extended out of the pump top to the rev-counter. A small ribbed cover concealed the pump and gave easy access for adjustment of its control cable linked to the throttles.

Because the pump, and the rev-counter, were driven by the gearbox itself neither was turned if the clutch was lifted. Thus it was important to shift into neutral during traffic halts and this was made easy by the usual Suzuki gearchange that went from second to neutral in one pedal move. When the traffic moved off the oil pump drive was interrupted while the clutch was raised and also the rev-counter drive so that instrument could not be used to judge engine speed on take-off.

The lubrication system was a little more extensive than on the 250 with oil supplied to the rear of the cylinders as well as the big ends. Each supply line contained a check valve to prevent the oil flowing back, this being a usual fitment with the system, and the idea of a cylinder feed had already been tried on the T200.

The chassis which carried this engine unit was much as the 250 with duplex cradle frame, telescopics, pivoted rear fork, hydraulically damped suspension, wire spoked wheels and drum brakes. The rear fork was long as was the dualseat but the riding position was fine. Despite the fork length the handling was good for the era and in other respects the model was up to the mark with diaphragm fuel tap, turn indicators, passenger grab handle, mirrors and centre and prop stands. Speedometer and rev-counter were no longer built into one assembly but were separate instruments mounted side by side.

For riders who preferred the older way the gear change shaft was extended out on the right so the pedal and rear brake could be swapped over. Another special feature was the venting of the float chambers which was taken to the carburettor body intake. This gave automatic altitude compensation and Suzuki called the system homo-pressure.

1968 brought a further twin, the T305, which was a T20 bored out to 60 mm and 305 cc. The compression ratio went down to 6·68:1 and the power up to 37 bhp at 7500 rpm which gave it a useful increase on the 250. It retained all the features from the smaller models such as oil pump, 6-speed gearbox and coil ignition while the chassis was the same. It was really an interim model for it was replaced during 1969.

That year saw changes and new models in the twin range with the largest becoming the T500–II with cast-in cylinder liners and smaller 32 mm carburettors in place of the earlier 34s. The T20 went but in its place came the T250, much the same but improved with three more horses to 32 bhp at 8000 rpm on a 7·5:1 compression ratio.

Engine construction of the T250 remained very much as the T20 but there were some changes, the most obvious being the oil pump drive. The pump itself went on top of the crankcase, as on the T500, but the drive was different. It still came from the kickstart gear but this was now paired with another spur gear which meshed with a small pinion above and forward of it. This pinion was cut on a cross-shaft which had a skew gear at its inner end and this in turn meshed with another cut on a short vertical shaft. This latter shaft sat in a recess in the top of the crankcase which was covered by a round plate held by three bolts and which supported the shaft end and carried the oil pump.

A small cover kept road dirt off the pump but allowed the control cable to connect to it and its supply and output pipes to run to and from it. As on the 500 each output pipe fed one big end bearing via an outer main and the rear piston face on the same cylinder. The centre main continued to be supplied from the transmission oil.

The transmission itself also changed with a small variation in the primary drive ratio and changes in the gearbox internal ratios. The gear selectors became four in number mounted on two cross-shafts and the positive stop mechanism incorporated a brake to slow the gears when the gearbox was in neutral. The change sequence also became the same whether up or down so neutral was halfway between first and second as usual on other makes.

The T250 was followed by the T350 later in the year based firmly on the smaller engine. Bore was

Suzuki Two-strokes

Above **The 1977 GT500 fitted with several approved Suzuki accessories in café racer style**

Left **A GT250 being rescued by the AA—repair or just lost its number plate?**

61 mm while the stroke remained at 54 mm so the actual capacity was 316 cc. Compression ratio was 6·94:1 and power output 39 bhp at 7500 rpm. It was fitted with 32 mm carburettors in place of the 24 mm ones used by the 250 but in most other respects the two machines were the same.

The cycle side of both models was the same and much as the T20 and T305 but with new front forks with gaiters. All the expected features were evident with the twin leading shoe front brake, drum rear, full electrical equipment and nice Suzuki finish. The T250 was called the Hustler and the T350 the Rebel.

Another new model joined the twin range in 1967 at the bottom end of the capacity scale and took over the duties of the old S model. It was the T125 and at first was built as a smaller version of the T200. Power was up to 15 bhp on a 6·5:1 compression ratio and the appearance conventional. All this changed in 1969 when the machine became the T125 Stinger and only the capacity and power remained the same. The engine was in a new format for a twin cylinder Suzuki for the cylinders were nearly horizontal to the ground and the carburettors were downdraught. In other respects the unit followed their normal design with the same internals, primary transmission on the right, generator and points on the left and the gearbox, with five speeds, built in unit.

Bore and stroke were equal at 43 mm so the capacity was 124·9 cc, compression ratio was 7·3:1 and power output 15·1 bhp at 8500 rpm. Gear lever and kickstart were both on the left so copied the larger twins and the gearbox was the usual design. An oil pump went on the right driven in the manner of the T20 with the revcounter drive taken off in the same style.

The exhaust systems, one on each side were very different to those of the other twins and were styled to suit the Stinger's sporting performance. Each ran down from the port and then turned up and out to a point level with the port to form a U bend out from the machine. At this point it became a silencer and began expanding round a second corner to run back above the crankcase level. At the end of the silencer section it contracted back to the pipe diameter and then terminated in a second silencer. This alone was chrome-plated while the rest of the system was black with a chromed heat shield on the side of the first silencer, and very smart it looked too.

The frame of the little twin was rather like that of the TC120, a spine formed from tubes. It suited the machine well and the remaining details were standard build for the time. The forks had gaiters and the rear units covers while the style was fully sporting and very striking with plenty of plating and a vivid tank colour.

The Stinger was joined by the T90 in 1969 and this was built along the same lines and style but with a smaller capacity engine. Dimensions were 38 × 39·6 mm which gave 89·8 cc and the power developed was 10·5 bhp at 9000 rpm on a 7·5:1 compression ratio.

1970 saw the twin range settle down to Mark II versions except for the 500 which became the III and T200 Invader which was dropped. In 1971 the suffix changed to R and 1972 to J with cosmetic rather than mechanical changes. For 1971 in Japan the type numbers became GT250, GT350 and GT500 but elsewhere the old style remained.

1973 brought more extensive changes except for the 500 which became the T500K and continued as just about the most underrated machine of all time. The T125 and T350 were dropped while the T250 became the GT250K and a new twin, the GT185K was introduced.

The GT250 was only changed in two aspects from the older model, other alterations being minor or cosmetic. The change on the engine was the adoption of what Suzuki called ram-air cooling. This was a cast alloy deflection shield which attached to cylinder heads with revised fins and directed the air down to their roots. The shield was itself finned on the outside with the name of the system cast into each side and there was a strong suspicion that it owed more to the needs of advertising than engineering. For all that it did no harm and became a feature of a family of Suzuki 2-strokes.

The second major change for the 250 was the adoption of a single disc front brake which entailed a change of hub and revision of the fork legs. The disc went on the right with the caliper ahead of the fork leg and was controlled by a handlebar mounted master cylinder. It worked very well in the dry but sadly was appalling in wet weather, an aspect which continued nearly to the end of the decade before it was rectified.

All the Japanese machines with disc brakes suffered the same trouble and many were the cures used to try to get the pads to grip. Grooves, slots and holes appeared in all manner of patterns but in the end it was a change of pad material that solved it. It was a problem ignored by the makers for years because their prime market was the USA and there few riders used their machines at all in the wet. Suzuki for one added warning labels to the fork legs to tell owners that the brakes would not work in the wet but in the end pressure from the European market forced the issue and riders breathed again.

Aside from the brake the Suzuki performed much as its predecessors and ran far and fast without fault. Acceleration, handling, comfort and conveniences were all to the usual standard and the model continued to be as popular as always.

The new model was the GT185 and while it followed the general lines of the Suzuki twins in its construction it included some special features of its own. The cylinders were vertical rather than inclined but as usual were in light alloy with cast-in liners. The head was cast as one to cover both

The GT500 for 1976–77, in this case with special cast wheels and non-standard rear disc

barrels and incorporated a form of ram-air cooling with an additional plate fixed to its top surface.

Each barrel was held on four studs and eight nuts secured the head. Stub fitting was used for the carburettors, of which there were two, and for their hose connection to the barrel. The exhaust pipe was held by a finned ring secured by two bolts. Engine dimensions were 49 × 49 mm so the capacity was 184·8 cc and the compression ratio was 7·0:1. Power output was 21 bhp at 7500 rpm.

The bottom half was conventional Suzuki with needle roller big and small ends but the crankshaft details differed although it retained its pressed-up construction. In place of three mains and four seals went four mains and three seals, the centre one a double acting type. The change also affected the details of the lubrication system although the principles remained the same.

On the left end of the crankshaft went an oil seal outboard of the main and this bearing acted as the feed for the left big end. On the right the items were reversed with the seal inboard of the main which received its oil from the primary transmission. Between the inner flywheels went a third seal, on the left, and two mains in centre and right. The oil feed went between them to supply both and, via the right one, the right big end.

The oil pump went on top of the crankcase and was driven via a train of gears through the primary pair and idlers to the kickstart gear, then by a skew gear from the kickstart shaft. As on other models a cable connected it to the throttle and oil was supplied to the rear face of the pistons as well as the big ends. Unlike them the rev-counter drive was not taken from the pump but was driven separately by worm from the kickstart shaft to emerge from the top face of the crankcase aft of the pump but through its cover.

Other differences in the 185 occurred with the kickstart lever which was on the right and the clutch. This had its plates clamped together by tension springs which screwed into the centre at one end with hooks at the other to attach to cross pins. The clutch release dispensed with the normal quick thread and used a lever on a shaft which had a flat machined along part of its length. Rotation caused this face to move the pushrod and lift the pressure plate which incorporated an adjuster at its centre.

A 5-speed gearbox was used of the usual form with gear lever on the left controlling the barrel cam and the two selectors that moved on it, the third having its own cross-shaft.

The electrics went on the left end of the crankshaft and again differed. They reflected the old S and T10 models with a starter-dynamo unit and not the more usual alternator. The ignition system was coil with fixed timing and single cam to open each pair of points in turn.

The chassis of the 185 was as to be expected. A cradle frame with single downtube, telescopic front forks with gaiters to protect the legs, pivoted rear fork controlled by hydraulically damped spring units and drum brakes. The front was a twin leading shoe device and both it and the rear one went into full width light alloy hubs in wire spoked wheels. Slim front mudguard, deeper valanced rear, small chainguard, dualseat and neat tank gave it a nice line. This was helped by the tidy side covers which enclosed battery, tools, electrics and oil tank.

The machine was fully equipped with mirrors, turn indicators and a full complement of lights and controls. The fuel tap was just that, a three position tap operated manually and without the help of engine vacuum. Centre and prop stands were fitted and all in the machine was highly suited to use in traffic or for the shorter runs. The nice aspect was a top speed in the high 70s, the nasty one a consumption that could fall as low as 40 mpg if the throttles were kept open.

For 1974 the 185 became the GT185L and gained a disc front brake. It was joined by a smaller version, the GT125L and this was very similar

Above **The final GT250C of 1978, a descendant of the T20 and replaced by the X7**

Above left **The GT125 in 1978 with front disc, stripe styling and no ram-air**

in its basic format. The engine was based on a square 43 mm dimension so the capacity was as the T125 at 124·9 cc. Compression ratio was 6·8:1 and power 16 bhp at 9500 rpm. Like the 185 it had five speeds, oil pump and ram-air cooling but the clutch was lifted by a quick thread mechanism.

The major difference lay in the electrics as the 125 had an alternator with rectifier to turn the current into direct. Due to this it lost the electric starter and its wiring was a good deal different to that of the 185. In later years it was to forestall many who sought to swap engines over.

The 250 and 500 cc twins both continued with a change to an L suffix and for 1975 all four models took the letter M at the end of their numbers. 1976 was different for the two larger machines received a good number of modifications and all took a letter A suffix.

The largest became the GT500A and after nine years of production was actually changed to a noticeable extent. It gained electronic ignition, a disc front brake and a larger fuel tank while it lost weight, power and its steering damper. In all respects it was the same machine although time was now catching up with it. For all that it still offered a lot of motorcycle for the money with bullet proof reliability and easy maintenance.

The 250 was modified on the lines of the two smaller twins with a one piece cylinder head but without ram-air, four main bearings and revised oil system for the crankshaft. In addition the barrels were changed to provide two transfers on each side, the carburettor size increased to 28 mm and new gearbox ratios were provided for second and third gears. Other changes were a new air cleaner, the use of an endless rear chain, new and more efficient silencers, no cover for the rear suspension units and pillion rests on a sub-frame and not the rear fork legs.

The twins still had some time to go but not too much in their piston port form. They all ran on into 1977 with suffix letter B apart from the GT500A which dropped from the lists during the year. It left as it had lived, underrated by most but loved by its owners who had found it able to do most motorcycle jobs well.

Before it finally went the English importers offered it in a couple of modified forms to tempt the customers, the first being the fitting of cast alloy wheels and a disc rear brake. The second was given the name Formula 500 and was more extensively altered. The wheels were changed for rather expensive, but much lighter, Italian cast alloy ones and these had a single disc at the front and a drum brake in the rear. Most of the other changes came from the Paul Dunstall organization which had close ties with Heron Suzuki and comprised sports fairing, fibreglass seat base with new seat, rear-sets, revised foot controls and clip-on bars. Not one, but two steering dampers were fitted, one friction and one hydraulic, neither really necessary. It made a nice sports model to finish the line with.

In 1978 the models changed to a C suffix and the 125 moved its disc brake to the left. The 185 became available with cast alloy wheels as the GT185EC and the 250 reached the end of its line. It was rather noisy in its final years with pistons rushing past big ports so it was replaced by a new design, the X7, with port and reed valve induction, cast wheels, much less weight and much more performance.

The X7 represented a new generation of 2-stroke design and in 1979 was joined by the 200 cc X5 and its less highly tuned stablemate, the SB200. Before they arrived the GT185 progressed to its final EC form with cast alloy wheels but went from the range in 1979, replaced by a newer technology. The 125 hung on no longer and followed the same lines. It ran into 1979 still with its C suffix and with the option of cast alloy wheels as the EC model. Then it too went but was replaced by a reed valve version for a year or two.

So the range of Suzuki twin 2-strokes dwindled, pushed to one side by new environmental standards and the ever rising cost of fuel. They faded but refused to vanish completely from the lists but never from the minds of any who had ridden them and used their wailing performance. Whether 125 or 500 it was an exhilarating ride.

5 | Air or liquid triples

As the swinging sixties ran to their end Suzuki were forced to look for a new flagship to their range and this had to be a superbike. They had come very close with the T500 but that model, good though it was, lacked the last few mph expected of a top performer and failed to crack the rider's spine like a whip as it accelerated.

The twin was also lacking in visual excitement or grandeur, either, or both, of which were necessary for a machine to be considered a superbike by the general riding public. It slid unnoticed through the crowd and only the discerning appreciated how quickly it did so.

To the customer a superbike was a Honda CB750, a Kawasaki Mach III, a Bonneville or the first such machine, built before the term was devised, the big Vincent. Suzuki needed a machine in that class of style and power so they set to and produced one.

The result was, in essence, a simple solution. They took one-and-a-half T500 engines, added water cooling, styled it with multiple exhausts and launched the outcome at the Tokyo show in 1971. The machine was the GT750 and it was given the name Le Mans for the USA.

GT stands for *gran turisimo* or Grand Tourer and originally was used solely to describe a car able to tour in a grand manner. This meant not only a high top speed and excellent acceleration but also the ability to cruise effortlessly and quietly at speed, to carry driver and passengers in complete comfort, to accommodate all their

Above **The twin leading shoe drum front brake used on the early 750 cc triple**

Top **From the top its lights, turn, horn and pass with the choke lever in the distance**

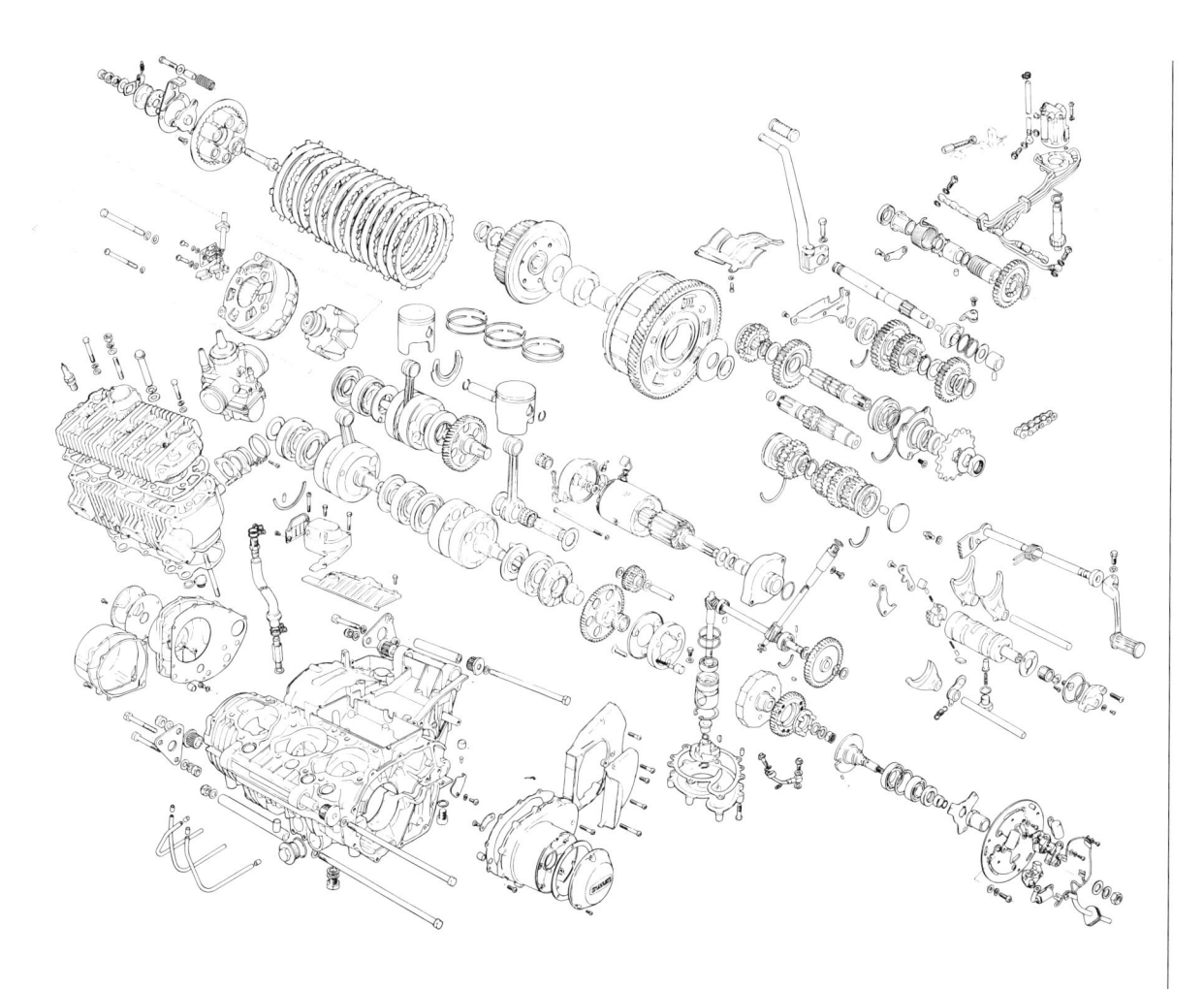

Exploded line drawing of the 750 cc triple engine unit with its water cooling and pump oiling

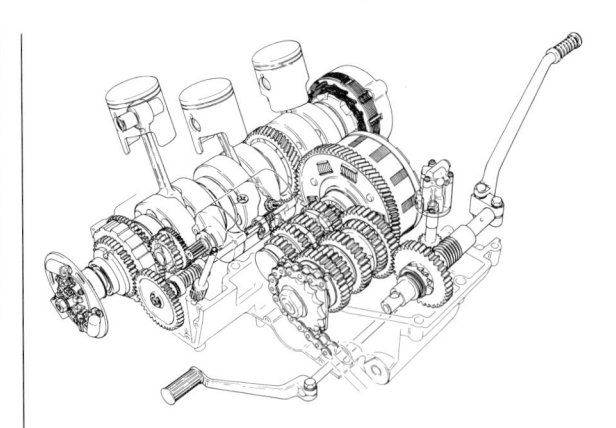

Above **All the GT750 gears for pumps, starter, ignition, rev-counter and transmission**

luggage and to do this in style so hotel doormen ran when the car hoved in sight. In time the letters became used more generally on lesser vehicles as an aid to promotion rather than an indicator of standards so they became debased.

It is to Suzuki's credit that they did set out to built a grand tourer rather than a super-sports model and the result merited the letters affixed to the typing. It was a large, impressive machine that ran very smoothly and offered considerable performance. To do this it swathed the familiar basic Suzuki 2-stroke with water cooling, a special pump lubrication system, electric starter, water pump and complete machine refinement.

The finished article was a trifle chubby, not really a fault for a grand tourer for width and weight gave it dignity. In truth it soon showed that the outer coating could be stripped off to leave a very lean racer and that this could be more than just competitive.

The heart of the machine was the engine which had three cylinders set in-line across the frame and inclined only a trifle forward of the vertical. Engine dimensions were old favourites at 70 × 64 mm which made the capacity 739 cc. The bore and stroke were thus common with the 250 single and 500 twin road and trail engines and also benefited from knowledge gained from the works motocross models which used the same figures.

The engine unit construction followed familiar lines with the gearbox built in unit with it, horizontal crankcase split through crank and gear shaft centres, primary drive on the right and final one on the left. In the detail construction there was a good deal that was different and new.

Left **1972 GT750 with leggy blond**

Right **Charles Deane testing a 1972 GT380 for** *Motorcycle Mechanics.* **Ram-air cooling and drum brakes**

Air or liquid triples

The crankshaft was massive but conventional in construction and lubrication. It was pressed together with four ball bearing mains and a total of five oil seals. The arrangement whereby oil was pumped through a main bearing, into a guide plate and thence into a big end remained just as always with the outer mains serving the outer crankpins. The centre pin was lubricated from its left but the main bearing to its right and between centre and right cylinders was shielded by a seal on each side. This enabled it to be supplied with oil from the transmission and outboard of the main bearing, on its right, was formed the output gear which took the drive back to the clutch.

By taking the drive in this fashion excessive clutch overhang was avoided, torsional stresses on the crankshaft were reduced and it made for a compact, correctly positioned gearbox whose oil could easily look after the primary gear pair and the fourth main bearing.

Both big and small ends of the steel connecting rods contained caged needle roller bearings and the gudgeon pins were hollow and retained in their pistons by wire circlips. At first, side thrust washers were only fitted to the big end but they later appeared at the small end as well.

The pistons were nothing out of the ordinary and their slightly domed crowns gave a compression ratio of 6·7:1. Due to the layout of the transfer ports the centre and left pistons were common but the right one was handed in the opposite manner in respect of the transfer cutaways. All pistons carried two keystone section rings and were taper and oval ground to ensure minimum clearance once they warmed up. This not only gave more power but also kept the noise down.

The cylinders were in one block in light alloy with the three liners cast in-situ. The design was unusual in that the block extended down to the end of the liners which did not protrude from its underside. The top deck was essentially open to give the coolant plenty of free passage to the head and the porting was straight forward.

Both inlet and exhaust ports ran out to a flange, the first with two studs to take the carburettor adaptor and the second with two tapped holes for the bolts securing the pipe clamp. The transfers were moved around the cylinder to allow them to overlap one another both in the barrel and in the crankcase. This allowed the use of large section ports without stretching the barrel centres, and thus the crankshaft length, to undesirable proportions.

The front and rear of the cylinder block was cast with small cooling fins running from top to bottom and these continued up and over the cylinder head. This, like the barrel, was cast as one piece in light alloy with the three combustion chambers, water passages and thermostat housing. The sparking plugs of the outer cylinders lay at an angle to the pistons while the

Typical rear view of the four silencers fitted to all the triples, this one being the 380

1972 GT380 engine unit with 6-speed gearbox and three-into-four exhaust

centre one was vertical. Due to this the measured ignition timing is always given as two figures as it is taken along the plug axis and the angle alters the dial gauge reading to increase it from the true piston movement.

The head and block were held down by sleeve nuts which located the parts and screwed to short studs in the crankcase. These major fixings were backed up by further bolts holding the head to the barrel and one nut on a short stud holding the barrel to the crankcase. One piece gaskets went into each joint face with three further O rings under the barrel to seal water passages.

The crankcase halves were massive light alloy castings held together by a multitude of fixings and with many added nooks and crannies for the extra items fitted to the engine unit. In other respects they were no different from those used for the twins and were finished off with outer covers on each side. Internally they were machined to take the ball races that supported the shafts, the pins and circlips that located the ball races and the seals that kept oil and gases in the right places.

The primary drive was by helical gears to the clutch with a six spring shock absorber built into the gear and clutch drum assembly to smooth out the drive. The assembly ran on a bush which in turn went onto a spacer fitted to the gearbox input shaft. Thrust washers restricted side movement and the clutch centre held the parts in place. The use of the bush in the assembly was so that, after its removal, the clutch drum could shift sideways and clear the crankcase enough to be taken off without the need to split the crankcase.

The clutch had eight friction plates, seven steel ones and six springs. The drum had a ring pressed over the fingers to prevent spread and both it, the centre and pressure plate were in light alloy. The clutch was released by lifting the last of these parts and the mechanism was on the right so had to pull the plate, not push it. It used three balls and ramps to reduce the operating load and the release shaft was drilled to act as a supply line for transmission oil running into the gearbox shaft.

The box itself was a 5-speed, all-indirect, crossover design with the two shafts each running in a pair of ball bearings. One gear on the input and two on the output were able to slide to engage the drive in each gear in turn. The free running gears ran directly on the shafts both of which were drilled for lubrication, the input one being plugged at the left end. Outboard of this went a blank seal in the bearing hole and this stopped any oil leaving via that route.

On the right the input shaft was sealed to the clutch release shaft which was in turn sealed to the outer cover. The output shaft carried the final drive sprocket on the left with an oil seal inboard of it and held in place in a plate secured with four screws. On the right the shaft drilling was sealed to a reservoir plate which caught the oil and drained it into the shaft centre from where cross drillings fed the free running gears.

Gear selection was typical Suzuki with a barrel cam beneath the shafts controlling three selector forks which slid on two cross-shafts, one beneath each gear shaft. A neutral switch went at the left end of the barrel cam and the positive stop mechanism at the right end. The pedal shaft ran across the box behind the cam to emerge on the left to carry the direct acting pedal.

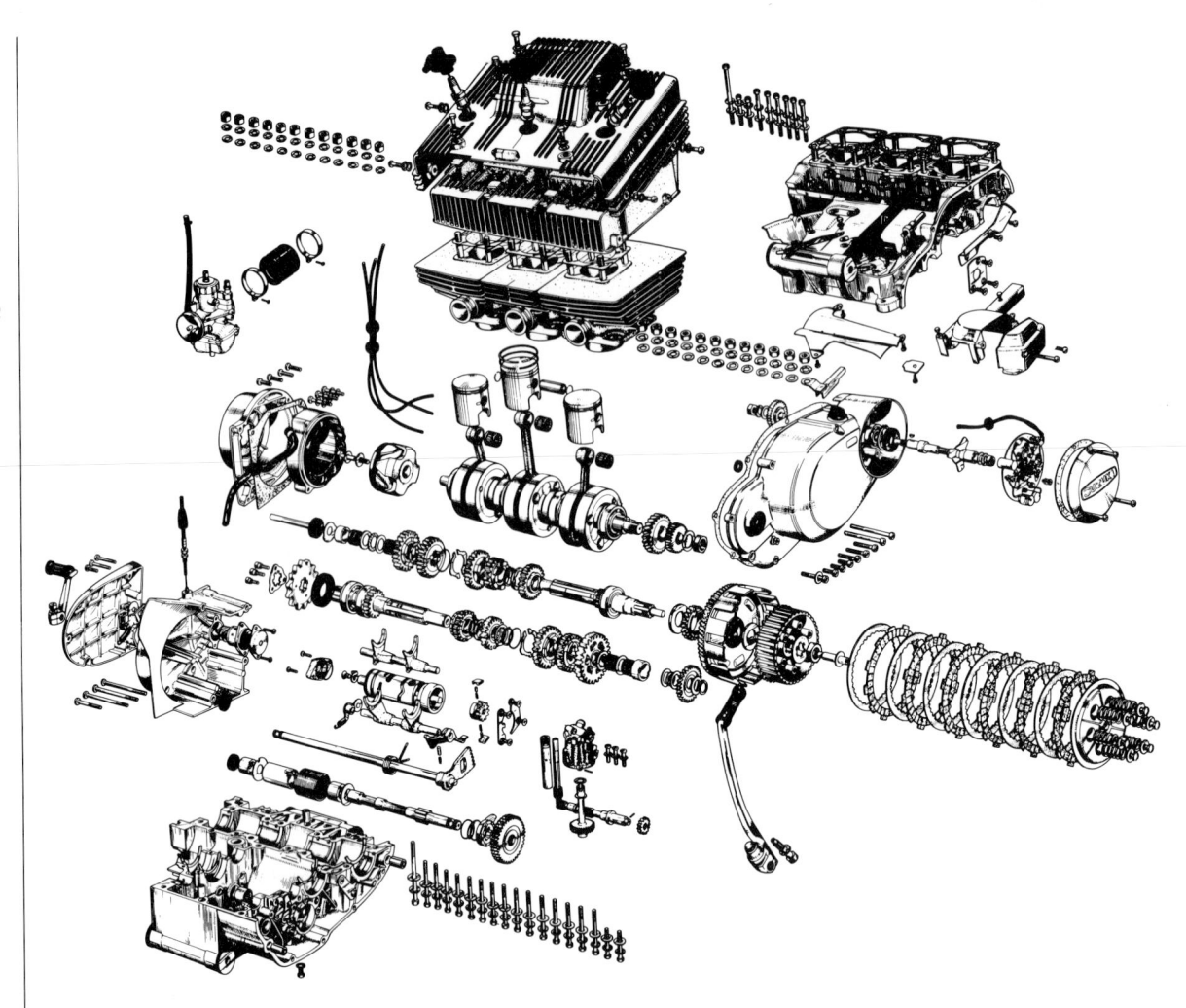

The kickstart shaft went behind the gear shafts and its gear meshed with the first gear train so the machine did not have primary kick starting. Otherwise it was the normal Suzuki mechanism and the pedal folded in when it was not required.

This was, hopefully, not too often as the machine was fitted with an electric starter. This was a straight forward direct current motor which was connected to the battery on demand by a relay controlled by the starter switch. It turned the crankshaft via two pairs of gears and a one-way clutch which was fitted on the left end of the crankshaft. The starter motor went on top of the crankcase in a recess where it was protected from the weather by a cover.

The end of the starter armature was cut into the form of a small gear and this meshed with one of the intermediate pair which ran on a hollow shaft supported between the crankcase wall and the left outer cover. The second gear

Above **Special 750 cc versions, the racing TR750 and the police Patroller with lights and siren**

Left **Middle of the range GT550 with drum brake and 5-speed gearbox**

Far left **The GT380 engine unit with its special ignition cam and oil pump drives**

meshed with a larger one that ran free on a caged needle roller bearing mounted on the crankshaft next to the left oil seal.

Outboard of the gear bearing the crankshaft was tapered and to this the starter clutch housing was keyed. Inside this went three rollers and springs arranged to form a clutch that acted on a diameter turned on the gear. This worked in one direction only so that while the starter could turn the crankshaft the reverse did not occur and the rollers tended to lift off the gear diameter under centrifugal force.

The starter clutch housing carried a gear locked to it and this in turn had a pin pressed into it to protrude out to the left. It was used to drive a shaft which ran in two ball races mounted in the left side cover and carried the ignition cam at its left end. The shaft was formed into a disc on the right and a slot in this mated with the pin. A rubber moulding between the disc and its driving gear damped out any oscillations or rattles between the two.

Ignition was by battery powered coil so three sets of contact points were mounted on a plate carried on the outside of the left cover along with their condensers and an access plate kept the weather off them. The three coils went as a unit on a bracket under the fuel tank and a key and a kill switch turned the system on.

The generator fitted to the GT750 was a three phase alternator with a field coil in the rotor. This fitted to the right end of the crankshaft and the

Air or liquid triples

109

A GT750 at the end of the assembly line in Japan and ready for a rolling road test

stator bolted to the crankcase with a light alloy cover over it. Aft of this a second cover enclosed the primary drive, clutch and selector mechanism with an access plate allowing the clutch adjuster to be serviced.

The gear attached to the starter clutch housing meshed with a plastic one fixed to the end of a cross-shaft which ran in a pair of ball bearings mounted on the crankcase joint behind the crankshaft. Two gears were cut on the shaft and that on the left was a worm which drove a near vertical shaft. This ran up in a detachable housing set in the top of the crankcase and drove the rev-counter. The second gear was a skew and the shaft it drove ran straight down to the water pump.

The pump was the impeller type and the casing for the water run was cast part into the base of the crankcase and part in a matching cover. The impeller went onto the drive shaft with a water and then an oil seal above it with a ball race above that. The race and the two seals were carried in a small housing secured by a single bolt and itself sealed in place by a pair of O rings. A short breather pipe took any seepage from between the seals and drained it out of the base of the crankcase.

The cooling system used a high percentage of an anti-freeze which contained a corrosion

The 1973 GT380 with disc front brake

The not quite similar GT550, also from 1973

Air or liquid triples

GT750 clocks, gauges, warning lights, gear indicator, ignition switch and radiator cap with de-pressurization button

inhibitor to protect the all aluminium engine. The system was of the forced circulation type with radiator, header tank, electric cooling fan and thermostat. The radiator was positioned across the machine ahead of the engine and was in aluminium. Hoses ran from the top and bottom tanks to the engine and a further hose ran up from the top tank to the filler cap. This cap maintained the system pressure, acted as a safety valve if this rose too high and allowed air in if a vacuum developed on cooling. It also had a knob which the rider could depress to release the internal pressure which was thus allowed to escape harmlessly before the cap was removed.

The rest of the water circuit was built into the engine with internal connections from the pump to the cylinder block base. A single pipe ran from the underside of the thermostat housing to the pump and acted as a bypass when the engine was cold. It was sealed by the thermostat as this warmed up and in doing this the latter opened the path for the coolant to flow up to the radiator.

A thermo-gauge unit was screwed into the rear of the cylinder head in the thermostat chamber and this monitored the temperature of the coolant. It was connected to a gauge mounted on the fork top for the rider to keep an eye on. Above the unit went a thermo-switch screwed into the thermostat cover and thus not influenced by the rising coolant temperature until the thermostat had opened. If the water became too hot the switch contacts came together and the cooling fan ran. This was fitted in behind the radiator to which it was cowled and the fan had four blades.

Engine lubrication was by the usual Suzuki CCI system with the oil pump driven by a worm cut onto the kickstart shaft sleeve. This was coupled to the gear on this shaft axis and thus rotated via the gearbox train. So, as with other models, the pump did not run unless the clutch was engaged.

The pump control was linked to the throttle and between it and the crankcase top went a manifold from which ran six delivery pipes. These connected to three points to supply the mains and big ends and at three more to feed to the rear of the pistons. The oil was carried in a tank on the right side of the machine below the seat and a level bubble allowed the rider to check its contents.

The lubrication system included a further feature known as Suzuki Recycle Injection System or SRIS. This was an arrangement where any oil that was not burnt and therefore drained down into the crankcase was forced through a check valve and a pipe into the transfer port of another cylinder. At first both left and right crankcases connected to the centre cylinder transfers and that case went to the right cylinder. This was soon modified so right case went to centre cylinder transfer, centre case to left inlet port and left case to right cylinder transfer.

The fuel mixture was supplied by a trio of slide type carburettors with clip fittings to the inlet stubs and the air filter body. The centre unit had a slightly smaller main jet than the outer ones and also a different needle jet but otherwise they kept the same settings. Fuel was supplied from the tank via a diaphragm tap which incorporated a reserve supply position and a filter.

On the exhaust side went an array of three pipes but four silencers which gave the machine a distinct appearance. It avoided the lopsided look of the Kawasaki triple and took on more of that of the Honda four. The outer pipes ran back into their silencers as usual but the centre one diverged under the engine to become two, each with its own silencer. The three pipes were coupled by cross tubes which fitted into flanges in the pipe side, these tubes being sited under the front of the engine and ahead of the split in the centre one.

The power unit produced 67 bhp at 6500 rpm and thanks to the smooth shape of the ends of the block and head, plus the water cooling, became known as the kettle in the UK. In truth it must have been a well watched one for it seldom boiled.

The chassis side of the GT750 followed a well established Suzuki pattern. The frame was a duplex cradle with a single top tube bracing the headstock to the tank rails and supporting the engine unit at front and rear in plates. A sturdy centre stand went between the lower frame tubes and a prop hinged out from the left one. The latter worked very well but it took muscle to pull the machine weight up onto the centre one.

At the front went telescopic forks with hydraulic damping and gaiters to protect the fork tubes from road dust abrasion. For the rear end there was a pivoted fork moving on bushes and controlled by units with hydraulic damping and 5-position preload adjustment for the springs.

The wheels had steel rims and wire spokes with tyre sizes of 3·25 × 19 in. at the front in a ribbed pattern and a 4·00 × 18 in. with blocks at the rear. Both wheels had drum brakes and at the front Suzuki fitted a twin leading shoe in each side of the drum. Their diameter was 200 mm and each cam was linked externally with a rod and a cable ran from the front cam lever up to the brake lever which had a compensator built

Air or liquid triples

The 1974 Amsterdam Show with various triples to the fore

into it. For the speed rider each backplate had an air scoop, but to suit the tourer these were blanked off although the plates doing this could be removed.

The rear hub, like the front, was full width and in light alloy. It contained a single leading shoe drum brake of 180 mm diameter which went on the right and was cable operated from the pedal, also on the right. A torque stay located the backplate to the fork leg. The rear sprocket was bolted to a hub with axial vanes and these fitted between shock absorbing rubber blocks set in the left side of the hub. The hub turned on a pair of ball races with a third in the sprocket hub but the wheel was not quickly detachable and the one spindle ran through the complete assembly from one fork leg to the other.

With two silencers on each side and an endless final drive chain the thought of a rear wheel puncture could take on a whole new meaning.

The wheels were guarded by chrome plated mudguards and that at the front was braced by two stays on each side. At the rear the mudguard had a valance so was self supporting from behind the sub-frame.

The fuel tank looked massive but this was a little deceptive as under it went the top end of the cooling system so the capacity was 17 litres or 3·7 Imperial gallons. The filler cap was hinged at its forward edge with a latch at the rear so it could be flicked up with ease. It gave a good sight of the contents which aided when refuelling. Ahead of the cap went a hinged flap and this came up to reveal the radiator cap with its red finished safety knob in the centre. A single tap went on the left with a diaphragm moved by engine vacuum to open the fuel flow. Tap positions were on, reserve and prime when fuel flowed even if the engine was not running.

The oil tank on the right was matched by a cover on the left and behind this went a panel carrying rectifier, voltage regulator, starter solenoid and turn signal relay. In the middle went the 12 volt battery with the air cleaner in front and engine oil filler cap behind.

Further forward the radiator was enhanced with side embellishments and protected by crash bars which ran round it and in front from top to bottom. The chainguard was less impressive as it left the chain exposed to the elements but the seat was massive with ample room for rider and passenger. The latter had a grab rail provided behind the seat, which hinged up for battery

The GT750 in 1974 with twin front discs and revised tank lining

access, and footrests mounted on the silencer supports.

The electrical system was very comprehensive with the sole omission of a front brake stop light switch on the standard machine. This was wired for and fitted to machines supplied to North America but other countries had the rear brake switch only, a Suzuki foible that lasted for many years. In other respects it was all there with headlight, massive taillight with twin bulbs, turn indicators and side reflectors.

The handlebars were neither too wide nor too high and carried a mirror on each side. The controls were normal levers but with a little too many electrics for the left hand. On the right went the kill switch and starter button but on the left things were more congested with lights, dip, turn, flash and horn switches all in one block. As with other Suzukis it was all too easy to switch the lights off instead of just dipping the headlight which led to confusion all round.

The instruments were speedometer with total and trip odometers, a rev-counter and a temperature gauge scaled C and H and normally never to get much past the centre mark between the two letters. Warning lights were minimal with just turn signal, neutral and high beam being fitted.

All told it was an impressive package and very quickly the reports came back that it went in the manner expected, not a super sports machine but a real *gran turisimo*, able to run at a smooth high speed for hours on end—or until fuel was needed. Top speed was around 110 mph but this was much less important than the wide spread of power and the easy way it ran down the highway. Handling and brakes were not at all bad either although the latter did require a heavy hand to get results. The engine was basically quiet aside from the primary gears and the four silencers kept the exhaust very well muted. Truly the 750 earnt its GT lettering.

Suzuki were not a firm to rest on their laurels and by early 1972 the 750 was not only on sale

Above **Instrument panel for the GT380 from 1974 with useful gear position indicator**

Top **The complete 1974 GT380**

but accompanied by another triple, smaller and air cooled but with one more gear in the box. And that in turn was rapidly followed by a third triple with a capacity that fell between the two others.

The two new triples had much in common in their basic design but varied in detail by a surprising amount. At first glance one seemed to be a bored version of the other less one gear but in fact the drives to the ignition cam, revcounter and oil pump all differed as did the starting arrangements and even the clutch release.

The smaller model was the GT380 and based on a square dimension of 54 mm so the capacity was 371 cc. Compression ratio was 6·7:1 and power produced 38 bhp at 7500 rpm. The general construction followed the lines set by the twins and the 750 so the crankshaft was pressed together with a total of six mains and four oil seals arranged so that oil could be pumped into the three big ends via the mains. The end main on the drive side was lubricated by transmission oil.

Big and small ends were caged needle rollers and the pistons were of the usual form but with

The middle triple in 1974; rev-counter drive is from crankshaft, note linked exhaust pipes

Air or liquid triples

117

a keystone top and plain second ring. The cylinders were separate and cast in light alloy, each with a cast-in liner, and held by nuts on four short studs screwed into the crankcase. On the inlet side a stub was provided to take a short adaptor hose which clipped to it and the carburettor. The exhaust port ended in a flange with a pair of bolt holes for securing the finned clamp while the rest of the system was as on the 750 with three pipes feeding into four silencers, two on each side.

Three head gaskets were used but only one head for this was cast in light alloy as one with more nuts on studs holding it down. It was well finned and onto it went a cast ram-air shield whose line and side fins ran parallel to the ground unlike the cylinder fins which followed the small inclination of the barrels.

In the lower half a helical gear on the right end of the crankshaft drove back to the clutch. Outboard of it went a spur gear and this meshed with a nylon counterpart mounted on the end of a shaft which ran in ball races fitted into the primary drive cover. The end of this shaft carried the ignition cam and to the cover was bolted a plate with the three sets of contacts all hidden by an outer cover. On the left end of the crankshaft went the rotor of a field coil alternator with the stator bolted to the crankcase and a cover enclosing the assembly.

The clutch contained six each of friction plates, steel plates and springs assembled into the drum and lifted by a quick thread worm on the left. The drum carried a gear on its back which meshed back to the kickstart to give primary starting. That last gear also meshed with a small pinion below it on a cross-shaft. This had a worm at its centre which drove the oil pump via a vertical shaft and a skew on the left to drive the rev-counter. The pump fed mains and cylinders as usual and the lubrication system had the SRIS as on the 750 with each sump feeding into a transfer port.

The gearbox contained six speeds and followed normal Suzuki practice in its details. The

Left **Rear view of a 1975 kettle showing off its four silencers**

Above right **The 1975 GT380. Smallest triple engine differs from 550 in more ways than are first apparent.**

Right **A 1975 GT550 out on test**

Air or liquid triples

Another cheesecake shot; this is of a 1976 GT750, the lady is not named

assembly and the engine went into a horizontally split crankcase and this was held in the frame at three points.

The chassis of the 380 was very much as the 750 but reduced in scale a little. In deference to the machines lower weight and speed only a single front brake was fitted but it remained a twin leading shoe device. Otherwise it was the same again with telescopics, pivoted fork. dualseat, oil tank, side cover and full equipment and instrumentation.

The machine proved to be very smooth and able to offer 100 mph, just. It also drank fuel rapidly if the performance and acceleration were used as intended but this was what the machine was designed for. The handling was acceptable but weaved when pushed hard and the minor controls would have been improved if the light switch had been moved from left to right. The worst aspect proved to be the front brake which was prone to fade if used too much. That aside the GT380 was a fast and exciting machine to ride and able to cover the ground quickly.

The GT550 which soon joined it was considerably quicker and much more exciting. The power output was up to 50 bhp at 6500 rpm and came from engine dimensions of 61 × 62 mm, a capacity of 544 cc, and a compression ratio of 6·8:1. The construction of the basic engine was as the 380, as was the alternator, but the ignition cam drive differed and was more as the 750 but on the right. It still had a separate shaft mounted in the primary drive cover but this was inline with the crankshaft and pin driven from the primary drive gear. The shaft had a further job to do as it also incorporated a worm to drive the rev-counter so the cable for this came from the front of the cover and not the rear of the crankcase as was more usual on a Suzuki.

The clutch, like that of the 380, incorporated a six spring shock absorber in the drum and had the same number of springs and friction plates. There was one less steel plate as the inner part of the clutch centre was machined to do this duty and the clutch release was by a ball and ramp mechanism on the left.

Only five speeds went into the gearbox so there were three selectors and not four as in the smallest triple and the remainder of the mechanisms was stock Suzuki. The kickstart gear meshed with the first gear pair so the box had to be in neutral before the pedal was used and coupled

Top prize in a 1976 *MCN* competition, this Apple custom job on a 750 was presented to the winner by Henry Cooper

121

Suzuki Two-strokes

Left **One of the three Suzuki triples which won the Maudes trophy for the firm**

Right **The Dunstall GT750 for 1976 with touring accessories including screen and tank. Paul Dunstall is proud of his work**

Below **The 1976 GT380 not much changed from its launch**

122

Air or liquid triples

to the gear was a worm which drove the oil pump via a vertical shaft. The pump, as usual, fed mains and barrels while the SRIS was used as on the 380.

Neutral kickstarting was no real problem for the 550 as it was fitted with an electric starter as well. This was a direct current motor mounted under the crankcase in a recess but unlike the 750 it was geared to the clutch drum. The one way roller drive fitted behind the clutch gear with the usual three spring loaded rollers and the gear meshed via an intermediate pair to the motor armature.

The chassis of the 550 was nearly the same as the 380 but differed in some respects. Although the two machines looked so similar they had different lengths and wheelbases. The 380 had smaller section tyres than the other two triples but the 550 had the dual, twin leading shoe front brake as used by the 750. All three models shared the same rear drum although with different rear sprockets.

Both the smaller triples were given names for the USA market with the 380 known as the Sebring and the 550 as the Indy. It proved to be a quick machine that guzzled fuel but gave its rider a time to remember. One tester called it a virago and it was not a machine for docile, easy travel but one that required to be ridden hard, fast and far.

For all that the Suzuki triples were all seen as the 750, a tourer, maybe a semi-sports tourer, but never anything more. The word, right or wrong was that if you wanted a triple that really went you shopped at Kawasaki who gave you raw, unadulterated performance and adrenalin pumping excitement with lots of power and a weaving chassis. The Suzuki was looked upon as more refined, less temperamental, maybe better at the job of going from point to point but sadly, because of this, boring.

The one major excitement, lack of brakes, was dealt with on the K models introduced for 1973 as all three were fitted with disc front brakes, the 750 with dual discs. These followed the usual Suzuki pattern with the single discs on the right and the calipers ahead of the fork legs. They worked well in the dry and badly in the wet so in a year or so the legs carried the famous warning sticker. This read 'Caution—braking performance at beginning of the application may change with wet brake disc' and a politician could hardly have devised more evasive words.

The 750 had other changes introduced the next year, 1974, with the fitment of constant velocity carburettors and, due to these, a new air cleaner box. This fitted behind the units to which it was connected by hose and the filter element slipped in easily from the left side. The cooling fan became an optional fitting as it was not really needed in many countries provided the system was working as it should. The gearing was raised by changing both the final drive sprocket pair and by lowering the internal top gear ratio by changing the pinions. To help the rider a gear position indicator was fitted below the instruments and proved to be a useful addition. The 550 also changed the final drive sprockets and the top gear internal ratio but the overall effect was to leave the ratio between engine and rear wheel the same. The carburettors also changed to constant velocity types but only for the one year when the models all had an L suffix.

1975 brought the M suffix and changes for the two larger models. Both put out more power and the 750 did this with a raised compression ratio while the 550 was fitted with new barrels with chromed bores. In each case the power went up by 3 bhp, the 750 to 70 and the 550 to 53 at an increased engine speed of 7500 rpm. That year the forks all lost their protective gaiters, no steering dampers were fitted and the three exhaust systems were made separate without any cross-connections.

The 750 had a further rise in its overall gearing for 1976 when the machines took an A suffix and also altered the internal ratios for second and third gears by a small amount. 1977 brought the

B suffix and this was the last year for the 750 and 550 which had to give way to a new wave of 4-strokes. The 380 ran on for a year or two without alteration but it too went at the end of 1979 to halt the line of Suzuki triples.

The machines went as they had lived, rather underrated but eyecatching, especially in the high, wide and handsome 750 form. They had proved their reliability the hard way late in 1974 when Suzuki attempted to win the prestigious Maudes Trophy, an award only given by the ACU to a company if the certified test it carried out was of sufficient merit. The trophy had been presented by George Pettyt of Maudes Motor Mart, Exeter to encourage demonstrations of reliability and economy, easy service and spares that fitted back in 1923 and had at first been known as the Pettyt Cup.

Some very arduous, long distance tests were conducted to try to win it and from the start Norton were very successful, taking it four years in a row. It then went to Ariel and moved among English firms in the 1930s to finish at Triumph in 1939. BSA took it from them in 1952 and held it for a decade until Honda won it in 1962. They kept it one year longer until 1973 when BMW took it by running two flat twins round the TT circuit for a complete week.

Suzuki decided to let an example of each of the triples do three laps of the coast of Great Britain using the Beamish premises at Brighton on the south coast as a starting point. As always with such ventures there were dramas and problems along the way but the machines all completed their task and in due course Suzuki were awarded the massive trophy.

So the triples bowed out on a highlight, mourned by many owners, but victims of their own thirst, the ever rising cost of fuel and the ever increasing emission controls of the world.

6 Rotary motion

Jitsujiro Suzuki, president of the Suzuki Motor Company with the rotor from the RE5 engine. It was not to be a happy story

There have been many attempts to oust the piston engine from its role of prime mover by some form of rotary motion. Few have progressed further than an idea on paper and only one, the Wankel, reached beyond the prototype stage into real production. Its form dated back to 1954 and its origins were the NSU company in Germany.

At that time they built and raced motorcycles with considerable success and went on from there to record breaking with a machine known as the flying hammock. This was extremely low with the rider laid on his back to reduce height and frontal area while full enclosure resulted in a very low drag coefficient and a very slippery shape. Thus it needed little power to break records although the acceleration was very gentle. One such machine was fitted with a supercharged 50 cc engine and that blower was based on the principle later adopted for the Wankel engine.

The basic scheme utilized a triangular rotor with curved sides turning in a double cylinder shape so that all three corners of the rotor continually touched the sides. This was done by mounting the rotor on a bearing on the output shaft but offset from the shaft's centre to run as an eccentric. The rotor was geared internally on its centre and meshed with a fixed gear concentric with the output shaft.

The resultant movements of the rotor tips were quite predictable and followed a trochoid curve, this being the path traced out by a point on a wheel as that wheel rolled along rather than just rotated. A three-sided rotor generated a form which looked like a figure eight outline with two internal chambers joined together and on the same lines four sides gave three chambers, five sides four chambers and so on.

Only three were needed to give the working cycle of the internal combustion engine but it took a decade to solve the problems of sealing and general knowledge of the principles involved. There were other difficulties as while it was easy to balance the rotor it still continued to move in a complex manner with violent accelerations. It proved necessary to pass oil through the rotor to cool it and so rapid were the rotor movements that any debris in the oil could punch its way out through the rotor sides.

The engine was similar to a 2-stroke in that it had ports and its performance depended on their size and position. However the gearing between rotor and shaft plus the unusual manner of operation led to arguments as to the correct swept volume of engine. NSU persevered with these problems and in 1964 were able to launch a car with the Wankel rotary engine. In later years the Japanese firm Toyo Kogyo bought a license from NSU and used the principle in their Mazda cars while other firms took options and built prototypes.

In 1970 Suzuki took the plunge and signed an agreement with NSU for a license to build rotary engines but it was nearly three years before the results became hardware and a machine. The model was called the RE5, short for rotary engine and 500 cc, after an initial listing as RX5, and the aim was to make a sophisticated, smooth sports tourer able to better the grand touring image of anything else. The use of the Wankel engine was to demonstrate that Suzuki were stepping ahead of the crowd with the newest technology and offering the highest levels in comfort and equipment. As the RE5 was to be the company's technical flagship and supreme tourer the GT750 was uprated a little to shift it more to the sports market and thus avoid a clash of Suzukis striving for a common customer.

In truth the GT750 was never able to wear the sports image too comfortably and the RE5 ran onto some hidden rocks.

All this was well into the future when the first photos were published late in 1973 following a home launch at the Tokyo show that year, only two years after the 750 had appeared. It was a little while before any real details were released but in late 1974 the press was given a run on the new machine from Los Angeles to Phoenix in shifts. In the main they liked what they rode, finding it fast and smooth.

The appearance was a mixture of old and new for the chassis was up-to-date but otherwise familiar in tubing with teles, swing-arm and all the usual things in the usual places. The engine was totally different and something of a lump.

The Suzuki rotary on show, in this instance fitted with rear lamp from a triple

It had no shape a motorcyclist would know, no cooling fins and any number of covers and housings, none of which were in expected places or doing quite the job normally reserved for them. It was something of a mystery and the technical press of the day had quite a time trying to explain the odd movement of the rotor and why it followed that path.

Suzuki referred to it as the two-node, three-apex concept and it was well analysed by that time. However the behaviour and the mathematical proofs were complicated and a science of their own. From this work came the knowledge that the basic dimensions of the engine were the generating radius and the eccentricity. The first was the distance from the rotor centre to its tips and the second the offset of the rotor from the output shaft. The two combined to determine the profile of the chamber and the ratio between them set the maximum compression ratio of the engine, this rising with the first figure. In operation it could be reduced by recessing the rotor flanks.

The construction of the engine began with the rotor housing and its two sides. All were cast in aluminium alloy and the inner surface of the housing was electro-chemically treated with a composite material, nickel containing silicon carbide particles, which provided a wear resistant surface. The sides had their working faces coated with molybdenum deposited by spraying and between them supported the output shaft.

In the centre of the shaft length went the rotor bearing, offset to form an eccentric and onto each end went balance discs to counteract the rotor weight and which provided perfect rotating balance. The rotor itself had recessed flanks to set the compression ratio at 9·4:1 which corrected to 8·6:1 actual. Into the rotor centre went an internal gear ring and this meshed with a fixed pinion bolted to one side.

This gave the basic single rotor engine and the nominal swept volume was 497 cc although this was arguable. To this simple base was then added sophisticated and rather more complex systems to provide the mixture, cooling, lubrication, sealing and ignition. Together these added up to a fair degree of complication as all were rather special.

The sealing of the rotor within the working chamber and from one flank to the next was one of the major problems facing the engineers and the solution used called for many special parts. These were gas seals so had to contend with both pressure and temperature as well as the high speed at which the rotor tips slid along the housing wall. The tip problem was compounded by the need to seal the ends of the tips against the sides and the way the tip apex angled to the wall. It did not remain square to it but constantly changed as the rotor turned so that a tip radius was needed to cater for this. The tip seals, as did the side ones, had also to take up wear and accommodate thermal expansion.

The solution to these problems was achieved with three each of side, corner and apex seals which joined at the tip corners. The side seals ran in grooves cut parallel to the rotor flank curve and were forced out by backing springs. At the corners the rotor was bored to take a round seal also forced out by a backing spring. The side springs ran from one corner to the next with just a small end clearance equivalent to a piston ring gap.

The corner seals were slotted and into these openings were fitted the three part apex seals. The two ends were forced out radially by a spring and chamfered against the centre section so that it too was forced out while they went sideways

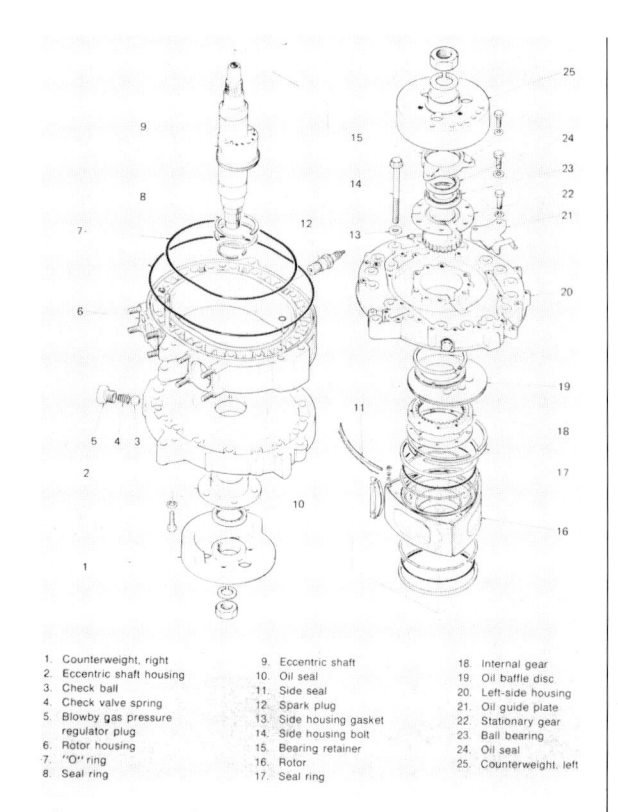

1. Counterweight, right
2. Eccentric shaft housing
3. Check ball
4. Check valve spring
5. Blowby gas pressure regulator plug
6. Rotor housing
7. "O" ring
8. Seal ring
9. Eccentric shaft
10. Oil seal
11. Side seal
12. Spark plug
13. Side housing gasket
14. Side housing bolt
15. Bearing retainer
16. Rotor
17. Seal ring
18. Internal gear
19. Oil baffle disc
20. Left-side housing
21. Oil guide plate
22. Stationary gear
23. Ball bearing
24. Oil seal
25. Counterweight, left

The not-so-simple parts that make up the simple rotary engine idea. Accessories are also complex

against the sides. This left a small gap above their ends but this vanished as the engine was run in. After that the end pieces sealed into the corner and took up housing wear.

This was not the end of the sealing problems as it was necessary to prevent the lubricating oil from forcing its way into the combustion chambers. To stop this no less than four sealing rings ran on the centre shaft and two more on the sides. The shaft seals were there to hold the oil in the main bearings that the shaft revolved in and were also needed to contain the oil fed into the rotor bearing. The side seals were each fitted against a spring and the chamber formed inside their diameter and between each pair of shaft

129

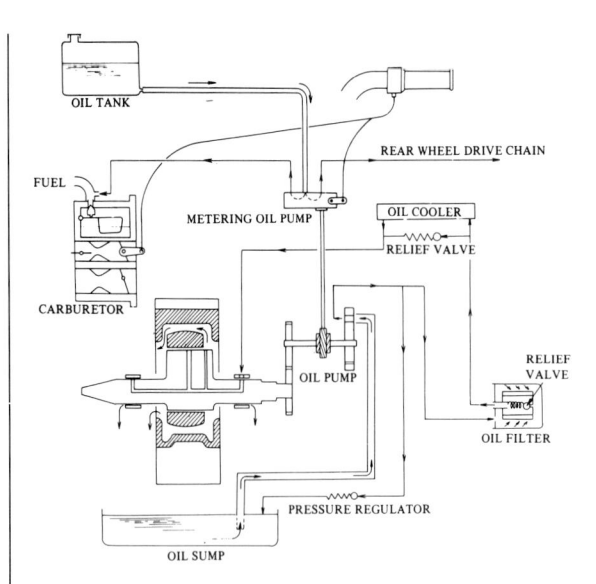

Twin oil pumps, twin choke carburettor and internal oil cooling add to the complication

seals acted as a reservoir for any gas that leaked past the gas seals. The resulting pressure was controlled by a blow-off valve and by keeping some in the chamber it could act to hold the oil seals against their working shoulders and improve their action. The blowby was taken to the engine intake so was then consumed and burnt.

The lubrication system was complicated by the jobs the oil had to do. First it was needed in considerable quantity and high pressure at the main and rotor bearings, second it had to lubricate the gas seals as they slid about the chambers and do this without contaminating the charge and third it was wanted in some large amount to flow through the rotor to cool it. To meet these needs not one but two oil pumps were fitted and two oil tanks used.

The main pump was gear driven from the output shaft and mounted on the right side of the engine assembly. The pump was the usual trochoidal design, in effect an internal gear type, and collected the oil from a sump built into the lower part of the engine. Its pressure was controlled by a regulator and the flow ran first through an oil filter. This was a full flow cartridge that screwed to the engine casing beneath the pump and from it the oil went to an oil cooler built into the bottom of the water radiator. Both filter and oil cooler had relief valves to ensure that any blockage would not interrupt the flow of oil.

From the cooler the oil went to the right main bearing and into the output shaft. This was drilled to supply oil to the left main and the rotor bearing with spillage looking after the internal gearing and draining back to the sump. The shaft drilling also fed oil to the interior of the rotor where it picked up combustion heat and carried it away as the oil passed on and out, back to the sump.

The needs of the gas seals were looked after by a second pump operated much as on a 2-stroke with its output linked to the throttle. The pump was driven from the same shaft that drove the main one and which was machined to a gear in its centre. It drove two shafts, one either side of it, with the upper connecting to the rev-counter and the lower turning the second oil pump. This was supplied from its own oil tank and the pump output went to two points. The first was the float chamber feed line where it joined the petrol and together as petroil they served the gas seals while the second feed was to the final drive chain.

While the oil dealt with some of the engine cooling the main job was done by water flowing through the rotor housing assembly. With water cooling came radiator, thermostat bypass, water pump, cooling fan, thermal switch and temperature gauge, much of it as used on the GT750.

The water pump was gear driven from the output shaft and went on the right behind it. The thermostat housing was above it with a hose running forward to the radiator base. The cooling fan was turned by an electric motor switched on if the temperature reached 106 degrees

Carburettor and filter trunking in front, oil sump below and gearbox astern but not a motorcycle shape

Centigrade and off again when it dropped to a level 100. The coolant was half anti-freeze and again one that was inhibited to avoid corrosion problems in the light alloy block. A header tank was included as on the big triple.

The coolant flow in the block was designed to even out the temperature gradient between inlet and exhaust ports which the Wankel layout dictated to be adjacent. The water mixture came in from the right to a chamber in the side housing from where it flowed across through the rotor housing to the left side. It was then circulated back and forth across the engine three more times, each time also moving further round the chamber until it had completed full circle and left the engine on the right.

By forcing the water to flow back and forth a better heat balance was obtained, there was less distortion and the induction area was warmed a little. Exhaust heat was further reduced by a very special exhaust. The hot gases emerged from the rotor chamber low down at the front and immediately ran into a well finned chamber. This fed two exhaust systems and silencers, one on each side, and these were attached by finned clamp rings. Each system was a double wall tube with an air gap between the tubes and this gap was kept ventilated by a ram-air intake at the front. Even these were special as they presented a restricted passage at first with trap doors which opened up as the machine

Intriguing instrument panel with flip-top lid unlocked by ignition key

went quicker to allow more air through. Black heat shields were attached to each silencer side.

The inlet side was also rather complex with two small primary ports and one larger secondary. These were fed from a twin choke, two stage carburettor developed by Mikuni and Suzuki and mounted on the front of the rotor chamber. The primary choke size was 18 mm and the secondary 32 mm and the carburettor had five separate circuits and a complex control linkage. This comprised a butterfly valve in the primary choke connected directly to the throttle and a port butterfly in the secondary port in the rotor also connected to the throttle but in such a way that it began to move only when the primary was part open. A secondary throttle butterfly went into the bigger carburettor choke and was coupled to a pressure diaphragm which sensed the choke vacuum and moved the valve according to it. This in turn depended on the engine speed and port valve position.

In addition to the three control valves the carburettor had a diaphragm type accelerator pump and more linkage for its cold start choke valve. This first connected to the primary valve to open that a little and was also coupled to a diaphragm which opened the choke a little as the engine began to pick up speed and run more steadily after a fully choked, fully cold start.

To fire the mixture once it reached the combustion stage was a single plug set in the appropriate segment of the chamber periphery. Producing the spark across its electrodes was a further complex system using a CDI with points control but involving two sets of contacts. One set comprised a pair opened by a two lobed cam which was geared to fire on each face of the rotor as it reached the plug with its compressed charge of petrol mixture. Along with this went a second set of points with a single lobed cam running on the same shaft as the two lobed ones. This fired every other chamber as it reached the plug so that it ignited the three of them once in two turns and not one. The later system switched in under the control of speed and vacuum sensors to avoid backfiring and erratic running during deceleration but normally the twin lobed system kept each chamber fired up in turn.

The system itself was battery powered with a converter to raise the voltage applied to the charge capacitor and a thyristor switched by the points to fire it into the ignition coil. The points and their operating cams were mounted as a unit outboard of the main oil pump and driven from the same shaft.

To complete the electrical equipment an alternator went onto the left end of the output shaft under a nicely styled cover. Below that was one with the filler cap for the main oil sump which ran across the engine beneath the main housing and was finned for cooling at the front. A needed feature as it was just behind the exhaust chamber and in a good spot to pick up radiated heat from that item.

The transmission of the RE5 was conventional aside from the primary drive and there was nothing very special even in that. Due to the distance between the output shaft and the clutch the normal gear drive was hardly a practical proposition so in its place went a duplex chain with a tensioner above the top, slack run.

The front end of the special exhaust system with finned expansion box and dual walled and vented pipes

From then on the transmission was taken from the GT750 with the clutch modified with a dual sprocket and the lift mechanism moved to the left so it worked through the input shaft. The gearbox was the 5-speed one from the 750 with the same internal ratios, change mechanism and kickstart only modified where needed to fit into the RE5 castings.

An electric starter was provided and was mounted above the gearbox behind the engine chamber. It drove the clutch sprocket via a two stage gear reduction with the pinion cut on the motor armature meshing with one gear of the intermediate pair. The second, smaller, gear of that pair meshed with a large gear mounted between the clutch sprocket and the gearbox with a roller clutch at its centre to transmit the drive when needed.

In all it was an impressively large engine unit and from it came 62 bhp at 6500 rpm. It was installed in a straight forward duplex tubular frame built on familiar Suzuki lines and fitted with telescopic front forks and pivoted fork rear suspension. No fork gaiters were used and only minimal top covers on the rear units. The wheels had steel rims and wire spokes with a

Suzuki Two-strokes

Above **Japanese launch of the rotary engined machine still with its RX5 badges**

Left **Oil filter, ignition points and water pump all outboard of the primary chain but again no motorcycle engine**

3·25 × 19 in. tyre on the front and a 4·00 × 18 in. on the rear. Brakes were double disc front and single leading shoe drum rear as on the GT750 and the chain that drove the rear was protected by a chromed guard fitted with a plastic tail to keep any errant oil away from the rider.

The radiator went across the front of the frame with a tubular crash guard round it and just behind it a cast curved intake on the left ran up from the carburettor. This was joined by hose to the air filter box which sat across the frame above the starter motor and just ahead of the side covers.

The covers were styled to the filter ends and lined to match the fuel tank on the first seen RX5. By the time the production models went on show the lining had gone to be replaced by badges which at first continued the RX5 typing, plus the word 'rotary', before adopting the final RE5. The earlier RX would have stood for rotary experimental.

Behind the side covers went the usual electrical equipment with battery, rectifier, regulator, turn signal relay and starter relay. Also the tools, protected by the seat lock which doubled as a helmet one. The seat was amply long enough and passenger footrests were mounted from the sub-frame lugs that also supported the silencers.

The tank was the same size as the 750 but styled in a different manner. Like the triple it had a hinged flap on its top at the front which locked down and under it went both filler and radiator caps. The fuel tap was opened by engine vacuum and incorporated a prime and reserve position plus a filter. Before reserve was needed the rider was warned of the impending fuel shortage by a flashing warning light on the instrument panel.

The panel was one of the features of the machine as it lay in a tubular housing set across the top of the headlamp shell. The housing had a side reflector set in each circular end and the round effect was completed by a transparent section over the instruments and warning lights. Aft of the housing and just ahead of the handlebars went a small panel carrying the ignition switch and a Suzuki badge.

The instrument panel had the 160 mph speedometer on the left and both trip and total odometers were supplied. The 9000 rpm rev-counter went to the right and was marked to indicate the low engine speed when the single ignition cam could be in use and from 6500 on when the engine would be reaching its speed limit. Perfect balance meant no vibration but the violent acceleration the rotor suffered generated

Rotary motion

135

heavy internal stresses which limited its speed.

Between the dials went a temperature gauge marked C and H and beneath that a blank space marked gear position. This would light up in red with the numbers 1 to 5 as the gears were engaged in turn and the switch for this was located at the left end of the gearbox barrel cam.

Below the gear indicator was a line of warning lights at the base of the panel with, from the left, three in red for low fuel, low oil level and low oil pressure. Moving along to the right these were followed by a green neutral, yellow turn signals and blue high beam. All these were automatically checked each time the machine was used as the first turn of the ignition key made the panel cover flip up to sit above the dials and the six lights come on. Moving the key round further turned on the ignition and the lights then took up their duties so that if all was well just the red oil pressure and green neutral would glow, the first going out as soon as the starter button was pressed and the engine fired up, the second when a gear was engaged.

The starter button was on the right bar with the kill switch and the left console carried the

Publicity photo of an RE5 in use, final version had 750 triple clocks and rear light

An RE5 pictured at the 1984 Italian GP at Misano. A very proud owner as most are

usual Suzuki grouping. This comprised the lights main switch, dip, horn and turn signals but lacked a headlight flash. The other controls were as normal with the choke lever mounted on the carburettor. The throttle movement was rather extended and needed two bites at the twistgrip to pull the butterflies fully open.

The headlight was a sealed beam type and conventional but the taillight was enormous and copied the instrument panel style. Thus it was tubular, set across the chromed mudguard, had all the rear facing area ablaze with red light and was fitted with side reflectors. The turn signals were also large and formed as spheres with half the shape acting as the lens so they were easy to see from all sides.

The dry weight was 507 lb and this climbed to around 570 lb when all the liquids were aboard and the machine ready for use. To hold it at rest there was a good prop stand on the left and a centre stand. The latter required a good deal of muscle and a degree of knack to get the machine up onto its feet.

The RE5 was an impressive machine, large and wide, and this had its effect on the performance. It ran up to 105 to 110 mph depending on the rider but took some time to get there. It took a firm hand on the awkward twistgrip to get it to jump off the line in anything like a sporting fashion and even then the acceleration was nothing exceptional. For a 500 it was a very good performance but the RE5 was not really built to a capacity class but as a large machine, able to run with any of the sports tourers. The ambiguities of capacity calculation for the engine were irrelevant for it fell in a class where power output and performance had to be marked 'enough'.

Unfortunately it wasn't for even the Suzuki triple was 10 mph faster while the CB750 was 10 up on that and the Kawasaki Z1 yet another 10 on at 135 mph. All accelerated better and all used less, much less, fuel for the Wankel consumption was very heavy. 35 mpg was about its best and that on imperial gallons while it was easy to lower the figure below 30 mpg. With the none too large tank this meant a fuel stop every 80 miles which hardly fitted the de luxe tourer image.

So the RE5 fell between too many stools. It was not fast enough for the sports rider, it was too thirsty for the tourer, it was too big for commuting and too heavy to move around easily. Road tests also showed up that its handling was nothing special and while the twin discs did a good job of stopping all that weight in the dry they suffered as badly as any others in the wet.

The strange engine put off a good few customers as well. In 1974 very few motorcycle units were watercooled so riders were used to seeing fins and missed them when they weren't there. The machines were bought by those who sought to have the new technological advance and also by some who enjoyed the smooth way the machine did its work.

Sadly for Suzuki most gave it the thumbs down, so often the fate of the pioneer. The large capacity, tourer market is small and tends to be conservative. It does not want to be stuck far from home with an unknown engine form that few understand and fewer have the spares and tools to service. Like other simple concepts, the ancillaries were too many and too complicated so they were not easy to set up correctly.

The Suzuki engine was a single rotor type and they never went on to build one with twin rotors. That, plus work to improve fuel consumption, might have saved the day if the result had kept its weight down. More power could have put the machine at the head of the performance tree but this would have meant something well in excess of 80 bhp then, rising to 90 within a couple of years.

An increase of this magnitude would have unleashed far more heat into the basic engine than it could have coped with without far more work. Such a move would have meant a complete new design and further very heavy capital investment with no real guarantee of getting more than a fraction back.

Suzuki made what must have been a very hard decision, to retreat off the limb they had found themselves on, mark the experience down as an interesting technical excursion and change direction. Before they did this they built the RE5 for a year or two up to 1977 and later models were modified a little. The rear light was changed to the one used on the GT750 and the instrument panel went to be replaced by the pods from the triple.

None of this helped much so the RE5 faded from the range in 1977 by which time the company was moving away from its traditional 2-strokes. With the sceptre of emission controls looming ever larger the firm switched to 4-strokes and in a short time had an excellent range of twins and fours for sale. Some became classics because of their bullet proof engines, others were to lead to the advanced Katana styling of the eighties but even then Suzuki did not forget their origins—the once humble but now so sophisticated 2-stroke.

7 | Motocross

Engine unit of the single cylinder 250 used by Kazao Kubo at the 1965 Swedish race

Suzuki works interest in motocross dates back to the early 1960s when they were also heavily involved in road racing. In that sphere they were successful in the smaller classes of 50 and 125 cc, technically interesting and prophetic in the design of their 250 but absent from the all-important 500. There was no sign of the success to come later and the expense of the small machines was hard to justify.

During those years Honda and MV battled for road racing supremacy in the two largest classes and the Japanese firm fought Yamaha in the 250, often providing the closest racing of the day. in such a climate an entry into the more prestigious events would have been expensive and unlikely to produce much in the way of immediate results. To be competitive meant producing the right hardware, having the right back-up and signing a top rider when most or all were already committed.

Suzuki decided to travel another way and to enter an area where their Japanese rivals were absent. Not that there was any shortage of European ones in the new arena but no doubt they saw them as obstacles that could be overcome. So Suzuki went into motocross, at first at home with some success, and then into Europe.

Their first foreign appearance was in Sweden in July 1965 and the rider was Kazao Kubo, a champion in his own country. He brought two completely different machines to try in practice, both of 250 cc, one a twin and the other a single.

Above **The twin used at the 1965 Swedish by Kubo and based heavily on the road T20 model**

Below **Engine unit of the twin used at the 1965 Swedish event before it was practised**

The twin was based on the T20 and had been his mount in Japan. Alterations to it for its new realm were fairly small with tyres, mudguards, seat and handlebars all being changed for more suitable parts. A small front hub with single drum brake was fitted and a pair of rather small expansion boxes arranged to run back and up, one on each side.

The twin, being based on a production engine, looked smooth and sleek but the single was a prototype and much rougher. It had a small and well finned crankcase, barrel bolted down on four studs and normal porting. The carburettor tucked in behind the cylinder with its air filter pointed to the right while the exhaust ran up on the left. It was this single with a 4-speed gearbox that was used in the race but Kubo fell after a lap and bent the gearchange so was out. He

Early days with the RH66, very much a prototype and still with a single loop frame

attempted to come to the line in the second race with another machine but was stopped by officials.

In 1966 Kubo was back with a single only and Suzuki took that first step along the trail to their motocross success. The machine was the RH66 and as far removed from later models as chalk from cheese but it set the pattern of a single cylinder 250. That first machine and the RH67 that followed it were primarily development models, built for Suzuki to find out how to go motocross racing at grand prix level.

Engine dimensions were 66 × 73 mm to bring the capacity very close to the 250 cc limit, compression ratio was 8·0:1 and the power produced by the RH67 was 30 bhp at 6500 rpm. It and the RH66 had much in common and were based on the same bottom halves. The first model had a very large but shallow cylinder head and on both the carburettor tucked in behind the cylinder. The exhaust system ran high on the right with a small expansion chamber and the rider was protected by a small heat shield on the 66 and a long one on the 67.

Only four speeds were provided on the early machines with the kick start lever folded in on the right. The chassis side kept to the same basis from the start but actual construction varied from year to year as the frame, forks and rear suspension were developed. Brakes were single leading shoe drum with the front one 140 mm diameter by 25 mm wide and the rear 150 × 28 mm.

The details changed in a number of areas from the 66 to the 67. The first front mudguard was smaller and less well supported although with a valance while the rear one went from a simple blade to a form that bridged the sub-frame to protect the air cleaner and ran on to a tail section incorporating the rear number plates. The fuel tank on the 66 was held by two bolts at the front but on the 67 had a new shape and a breather tube in its filler cap. The early seat was short and thin, the later one longer and fatter but from the

Motocross

141

The RH67 with the same basic engine as used a year earlier but in an improved frame

start the front wheel was a 21 in. Machine weight was 235 lb, very heavy for a competitive 250 and the wheelbase was too short at a touch over 52 in.

Those first two years taught Suzuki some of the pitfalls of motocross racing but by the end of them they knew they were not going fast enough to learn the real lessons. To do this they needed a rider who was fast, consistant and experienced in European racing. He also had to be dependable, able to analyse machine problems and faults, and be able to cope with them in the field.

The man they selected was Olle Pettersson from Sweden and at 30 years old considered by some to be past his best. Suzuki, in the person of team manager Ishikawa, thought otherwise for he saw the Swede as a top flight rider who could tell them what their machines lacked, ride them hard enough to prove the point, be steady enough to finish consistently and able to quickly push them to real grand prix level.

Pettersson spent 10 days at the factory evaluating the new RH68 and gave them his verdict, one based on the experience that had taken him to third place in the championship in 1967. It was redesign it. The machine was too short for Europe and only suited to the slow Japanese circuits. For

Left side of the RH67 which had twin expansion exhausts and was strictly a development machine

the faster ones half a world away the engine and footrests needed to be further back, the rear fork longer, the steering head angle changed and the frame so modified that it would be easier to start again.

Four weeks later Pettersson, back in Europe, received his new, revised RH68. All the changes had been incorporated just as he had asked for including many minor alterations in addition to the major ones. It was the best indication possible that Suzuki meant business and were determined to succeed. They were now able to concentrate on the motocross machines to a greater extent as their full works involvement with road racing in Europe had stopped at the end of 1967 although they continued in the USA to a lesser degree.

Pettersson set the style for the new RH68 by winning a heat on his first outing and the early season results were very promising. The machine proved reliable and the only real problem concerned the air filter. Tucked in just ahead of the rear wheel it could become blocked by mud flung from the rear chain so that during a muddy race the engine would starve.

This was easy to overcome but in July the team had a calamity. Pettersson crashed, broke his thigh and was out of racing for eight months.

Suzuki Two-strokes

Below Getting better, the RH69 which Pettersson took to third place in the 250 cc championship

Suzuki kept faith and the new RH69, which he had been due to test late in that fateful July was in action in March 1969.

The two machines were very similar and based on new engine dimensions of 70 × 64 mm which made the capacity 246 cc. The same sizes were much used for road and trail machines as well. The whole engine was new with compact crankcase, rack and pinion clutch lift, low level expansion box on the right and 5-speed gearbox. The gear pedal could go on either side of the machine, the kickstart was on the right and the weight, of the RH68, down to 211 lb. For the RH69 more use was made of magnesium and the weight dropped to 187 lb.

The power went up to 30 bhp at 6500 rpm for the 68 and the same at 7000 rpm for the 69. Not so apparent without sight of the full power curves was the change in band width for 1969. The earlier unit was peaky so the rider had to be shifting gears all the while to hold the revs up and could then find himself embarrassed by power when the going became slippery. By spreading the power out the rider could stay in

Left **April 1968 at the Belgian meeting with the RH68 ridden by Olle Pettersson**

Below **The RH68 pictured in January 1968**

Motocross

145

Success—Joel Robert on the RH70 in his first year with Suzuki when he won their first motocross title

one gear, ease the throttle when necessary for surface conditions and then open up again without trouble. Making the machine light and easy to handle meant that the rider could run at his peak throughout a tough grand prix with a reserve for any crucial last lap.

Despite the need to nurse his leg Pettersson was third in the title chase in 1969 and Suzuki knew they had a machine able to win the title. Early in 1970 they asked Joel Robert and Sylvain Geboers, who had taken first and second places in the 250 title in 1969, to Japan to try the RH70.

The new model was much as the RH69 but had a 130 mm conical front hub while the rear stayed the same full width 150 mm unit. The rear fork was fabricated from aluminium tube and sheet and the 6-litre tank was in the same material. Mudguards changed from it to moulded plastic and the exhaust system was tucked in more although it still ran under the engine and up on the right.

The Suzuki team dominated the 250 cc class that year and well before it ended Robert was acclaimed champion with Geboers second and Pettersson sixth with his work done. That year

Right **The 1972 works machines which brought more titles to Joel Robert and Roger de Coster**

Below **The man who laid the foundation for Suzuki's motocross success—Olle Pettersson**

Motocross

147

they also produced a 370 for Geboers to ride and that proved to be competitive from the start.

Before he joined Suzuki Robert had ridden for CZ and his team-mate for the 500 cc class had been the brilliant Roger de Coster. To cope with the Suzuki onslaught in 1970 he was moved onto the 250 but in 1971 he was back in the 500 class, not with CZ, but on a Suzuki. His brilliance was not to be denied and he dominated the class for several years to give Suzuki and himself titles in 1971, 1972, 1973, 1975 and 1976.

In the 250 class Joel Robert took his run of titles to five with wins in 1971 and 1972 but was not successful in 1973 due to injuries and other problems. That year the authorities instigated a minimum weight rule which halted progress in that direction so all the makers turned to the hunt for more reliable power. This was not too hard a task as for most circuits they had more than enough, the real problem was getting it to the ground and using it.

So a suspension war began with more and more movement for the wheels and better and more exotic dampers to control that movement for the full race period. It was a constant cycle for each increase in wheel travel placed higher demands on the suspension. At first this would sag during a race to leave the rider with little damping and condemned to a pogo-stick existence. Technology would catch up and solve the problem so the wheel travel was promptly increased once more and the whole cycle began again.

The use of a single spring and damper unit to control the rear suspension began in 1973 when Yamaha brought in their monoshock and this also gave some degree of rising rate to the suspension spring. By the arrival of the eighties such systems were common place with links and beams laid out by computer to give the desired results. The Suzuki system was called Full Floater and worked as well as any other.

Water cooling for the engines also came in around the same time, appearing first on the smaller engines. In 1975 a 125 cc motocross championship had been launched and Suzuki had made it their own. With their extensive experience they quickly produced a suitable machine and Gaston Rahier took the title with it. He repeated his victory in 1976 and 1977 and then went to Yamaha. With that make he battled through 1978 against the Japanese rider Akira Watanabi on the Suzuki and it was the latter who prevailed to become the first motocross champion from the Land of the Rising Sun.

The 125 Suzuki continued its winning ways with Harry Everts taking the crown for 1979, 1980 and 1981, and Eric Geboers for 1982 and 1983. Thus Suzuki had won all nine titles and had a total monopoly on the class. The 250 came back into the picture in the eighties with Georges Jobe taking the class in 1980 and 1983. In 1981 Neil Hudson won the rider's title by a very short head but Suzuki held onto the maker's one. The one year the 250 missed, 1982, the 500 fell to Suzuki with Brad Lackey the winner.

Thus by the end of 1983 Suzuki had taken a total of 21 motocross world titles with six wins in each of the two larger classes plus the nine 125 titles. More than anyone else by a fat margin and a far cry from those early models of 1965.

8 | Road racing

One of the 125 cc machines which ran at Asama in 1959. A model RB, it has tyres and air cleaner to suit the volcanic ash track

A Suzuki Diamond Free ran in the 1953 Mount Fuji race and this event, run on volcanic ash dirt roads up and down the mountains, was the first competition the firm entered. They did not win but their 60 cc machine did not disgrace itself running in the 90 cc class and in 1954 they entered a Colleda and that time they took first place for machines of that size.

In 1955 they ran at Asama but had to give best to the Yamahas but did have three machines finish. They missed the 1957 event but returned in 1959 with 125 cc machines which kept up with the Hondas until problems arose. Then the team began to fall by the way to leave one Colleda to finish behind four Hondas and ahead of two Tohatsus.

The Colleda used in 1959 was not a modified production model but built for the job, hence its typing of RB for racing bike. While it ran it was fast and encouraged by this and smarting from the indignity of defeat determined the company to do something about it. The decision was to follow Honda's lead and enter the 1960 TT. To this end they visited the Isle of Man in February and took a cine film of the entire circuit. They also persuaded Geoff Duke to give them a commentary and the resulting mass of notes gave them a notion of the problems and some ideas for solutions.

The race was not a success. The machines were listed as Colledas and the best position they gained was 15th after all that effort. They

149

Suzuki Two-strokes

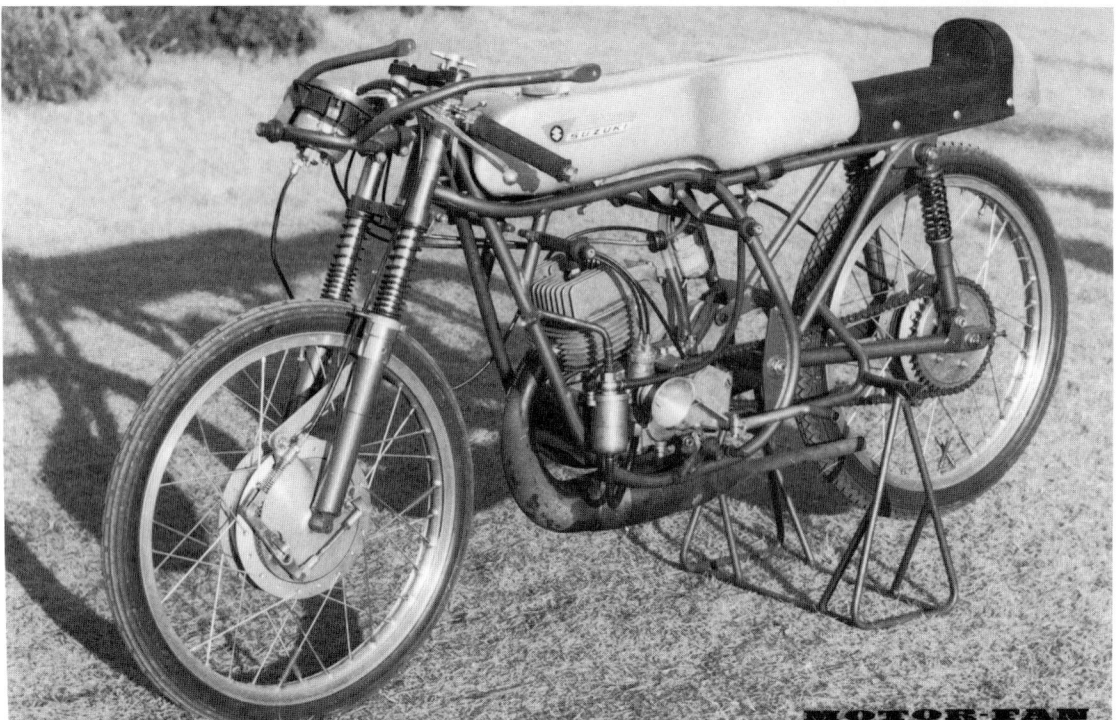

Road racing

Above left **A 1961 works twin under test near Hamamatsu Beach. Both 125 and 250 machines were built**

Left **The RM62 model which won the first 50 cc title for Ernst Degner and Suzuki**

Above **Paddy Driver in flight over Ballaugh Bridge during the 1961 250 cc TT**

151

Suzuki Two-strokes

Left **M. Itoh rounds Governor's Bridge in the 1962 50 cc TT in which he was fifth**

Above **Ernst Degner finishing third in the 1963 125 cc TT behind his team-mates, together they took the team prize**

returned in 1961 with 125 and 250 cc machines and ran into a season of troubles. Despite all the efforts of the team members and the recruitment of Western riders, retirements outnumbered finishes and at no time were the machines competitive. The Suzuki determination to succeed hardened more and they realized they just had to find someone who could lift their technical knowledge forward to a level that would put them on terms with Honda, MV and Yamaha.

They found that person in the shape of Ernst Degner who was both a very good engineer and a top rider with the East German MZ team. Negotiations took place in secret and in September 1961 he arranged for his wife and children to be smuggled into West Germany and then defected himself. By early 1962 Suzuki knew they had bought a bargain for Degner's knowledge of advanced 2-stroke technology gave them both power and reliability.

The team had also recruited two other top class riders during 1961, these being Hugh Anderson and Frank Perris. With Degner, who had come very close to taking the 125 cc title in 1961, they were a match for any other and looked forward to a better year. For machines they had a 125 cc single, 250 cc twin and also a 50 cc single for 1962 was the first year for that class in world title races.

The first two events of the season saw the team plagued with piston seizures but at the TT it finally came right for Suzuki and it was fitting

Suzuki Two-strokes

Above **Bertie Schneider on the 250 four during practice for the 1964 TT**

Right **Hugh Anderson winning the 1964 50 cc TT on the air cooled single with rear exhaust port**

Left **The four cylinder 250 being warmed up. Twitchy handling and prone to seizing, it won no classics**

that it was Degner who brought them success. He won the first 50 cc TT leading from the start and so gave Suzuki their first world championship win.

It was not to be their last for they were off and running with the years of struggle and disappointment behind them. Not that it was all suddenly easy for the 125 was no match for the Honda and was inclined to break while the 250 was not fast enough.

To compensate for these troubles the 50 was fast and Degner won in Holland, Belgium and West Germany. He missed the East German and Italian due to injuries sustained in a fall in Ulster and would never have crossed the Iron Curtain even if fit. He was accompanied by bodyguards in Finland and finally went to Argentine to finish second to Anderson and to win the 50 cc world title for Suzuki and himself. It was a good day for Anderson as he also won the 125 cc event which was the firm's first classic win in that class.

Events were even better for Hugh Anderson and Suzuki in 1963 for the New Zealand rider won both 50 cc and 125 cc titles and the 125 cc

Suzuki Two-strokes

TT. The firm also took the 50 cc TT again and this fell to Mitsuo Itoh who became the first Japanese to win a Mountain race.

At the last classic of the year, the Japan GP, Suzuki unveiled a new 250 with four cylinders set in a square form, a layout they were to repeat a decade later. The 250 caused a sensation in the press but although very fast it was temperamental and prone to seizure. Jack Ahearn named it 'Whispering Death' after a 1964 ride.

The 250 was water cooled with a 6-speed gearbox and in its early form rather lengthy. It was revised and lightened for 1964, and lost more weight for 1965 but a classic win eluded it although it did show the way to water cooling and the benefits of closer piston clearances and the extra power that resulted from them. Before water cooling was used for the smaller machines the team had one more air cooled year in 1964. It brought Anderson another 50 cc title and a 50 cc TT win but in the 125 cc class he had to bow to the new Honda 4.

For 1965 the pace hotted up with Yamaha joining in the 125 cc class while the 50 cc class continued with twin cylinder 4-stroke Honda versus twin cylinder, water cooled 2-stroke Suzuki. The 50 was a remarkable piece of miniature engineering with a 12-speed gearbox and minute power band that peaked at 16,500 rpm. Despite this it was not good enough to hold the Honda which took the title.

The 125 ran some 3000 rpm slower and managed with nine gears but these were enough

Left This TR250, based on the road model, ran in the 1967 production TT where one such was third in class

Below left **The TR50 production racing model which failed to make much impression on the racing scene**

Below **Sidecar ace Chris Vincent on a T20 in the 1967 500 miles race at Brands Hatch**

Suzuki Two-strokes

Left **The T500 ridden by Gordon Pantall and Brian Adams in the 1971 Barcelona 24 hour race**

Right **Barry Sheene at Brands Hatch in 1973 trying out the Seeley framed 500 twin**

Below **Pit stop at Daytona in 1972 for Jody Nicholas. Tyre trouble stopped him winning**

to take Anderson to his fourth title. He was less successful in 1966 but new recruit Hans-Georg Anscheidt took the 50 cc crown, a feat he repeated in 1967. Honda and Yamaha took the 125 cc class in those two years but right at the end of the period Suzuki produced their V4–125 which was capable of holding the similar Yamaha.

The new 125 had its origins from work carried out late in 1965. To increase power the engineers decided to follow the traditional route of more and smaller cylinders and built a 125 cc square four. It did raise the power but it also lengthened the engine to an extent that meant a larger frame and this upset the steering.

To deal with this they came up with the idea of building a three cylinder engine in the form of a square four but with the right rear cylinder removed. With the power taken out from this point a shorter engine resulted and thus a shorter machine. It was tested and although the power was up, the power band was very small and its eight gears not enough while the weight was up. The final solution was the vee-4 which was short and even more powerful producing 42 bhp at 16,500 rpm with a 1500 rpm band. The gearbox contained 12 gears and Stuart Graham used them to finish second in Japan on the machine's debut.

The three cylinder layout worked so well as a 125 that Suzuki built a 50 cc version in 1966. It was a complex unit and the power band was extremely narrow with the peak output little more than that of the twin. Thus the twin remained in use for 1967 but during that year rumours of a Honda 50 cc three prompted Suzuki to take another look at theirs. The result was a vee-3 with vertical centre cylinder and horizontal outers. The power produced from this incredible unit was 19·8 bhp at 19000 rpm and the power band was so narrow that 14 gears were not enough, more were needed. Thus although the specific power output was a record 396 bhp/litre the twin was faster round the circuits.

At the end of 1967 there were rumours of changes in the racing rules that would outlaw these very intricate miniature motorcycles. Then Honda pulled out of classic racing and later Suzuki followed suit. The machines were not all lost from sight as Anscheidt and Graham both obtained models and the former won the 50 cc title for the third time in 1968. His 125 cc twin went to Dieter Braun who took the world title in 1970 while Graham's 125 went to Barry Sheene. Despite its age it was still competitive and in 1971 Sheene came very close to taking the title and in this way began his long and successful association with Suzuki.

By then the FIM had decreed that a 50 was

The 750 works triple in 1972 with its special expansion box for the left cylinder

limited to one cylinder and a 125 to two, while neither could have more than six speeds. All the exotic machines vanished and racing became duller for a year or two on the grand prix circuit.

Elsewhere Suzuki were working on the basis that one door shuts and another opens. They wanted to boost their image in the USA so first off exhibited 50 and 125 cc twins in action. They followed this up by racing modified Super Six models, better known as the X6 in the USA, and these developed into the TR250 by 1968. This was not the first production racer for back in 1963 they had sold a few TR50 singles.

These had piston ported single cylinder engines carried in tubular cradle frames with telescopic front forks. Versions were built in super-sports street and motocross forms as well as for road racing but few were seen in use. Along the same lines had been the S40 with its single cylinder engine of 56 × 50 mm and 123 cc producing 15 bhp at 9000 rpm on a 7·5:1 compression ratio. The machine was built for street use and was in essence a road racer with lights.

The 250 was followed by a TR500 based on the T500 road model in 1968 and this was used by American riders Grant, Baumann and Nicholas up to 1972. One of these machines came to England in 1970 as something of a lash-up with the right engine and frame but road wheels and forks. The importers had got it for use in the TT but its high mounted engine and shortened wheelbase made it so traumatic to handle that its first rider, Stuart Graham, went home after one day. And Stuart was an ex-works rider for both Suzuki and Honda.

Malcolm Uphill rode it in the TT, fitted Norton forks and then crashed in the Ulster. It was that battered machine that Barry and Frank Sheene took over and with a Seeley chassis turned into a real race winner all over the UK.

In Europe the TR500 began to make a mark and in 1971 Jack Findlay won the Ulster on one, Suzuki's first 500 cc classic win. While they won no other races that year they did take second and third spots in the title chase behind Agostini and his MV. The 500, in water-cooled form from 1973 performed well enough in classics in that era and that year Findlay won their first Senior TT for them with two others on the leader board.

1972 brought a new racing machine, the TR750 based on the big water cooled triple. At first sight the touring GT was anything but a racer but its basic technology lent it to the job. Much of the width vanished when the alternator went and the crankshaft was cut off at the main bearing. On the left a shorter shaft drove the pumps and the electronic ignition, the clutch was changed to dry operation and close ratio gears were fitted. Fitting the expansion chambers out

The 750 in 1973 with a Seeley chassis, a very successful combination

Suzuki line up in 1974 with Gary Nixon, Barry Sheene, Cliff Carr, Ken Araoka and Paul Smart

of the way proved a problem but the real difficulties became apparent when the machine ran.

In its earliest form it produced 100 bhp and this was packed in a very light frame. For all that it was a big heavy machine and the handling was terrible. It was quickly termed the 'Flexi-flier' in tribute to this and its 170 mph plus top speed while at Daytona it ate tyres. Improvements were made but the team never had too much success in the USA although they did take much of the publicity in 1975 with the famous Sheene crash.

Barry had rejoined the Suzuki squad in 1973 with Stan Woods and really took to the big triple which he had installed in a Seeley chassis. The FIM F750 Cup went to him along with many other races and he continued to make very good use of the machine up to 1976.

Before then he rode the new Suzuki contender for 500 cc classic honours, the RG500. Work had begun on this in 1973 as a replacement for the tiring TR500. The aim was to win the world title and lack of money was not to impede the project.

The engine layout chosen was the square four with disc valves but with the drive from the crankshafts taken in a different manner to the old 250. It was built and tested ready for the 1974 classic season and Sheene came close to giving it a fairy tale debut when he finished second to Phil Read on the MV. He then began to hit development problems which brought him off more than once but it was clear to all that it was only a matter of time before the Suzuki was a winner.

It came in 1975 and it was fitting that the rider was Sheene who succeeded in Holland, and later in Sweden, despite his dreadful accident at Daytona earlier in the year. Then in 1976 it all came right for Sheene who swept to his first title and repeated this in 1977.

The RG500 was sold to private racers and proved very successful but in 1978 the factory had to contend with Kenny Roberts and his Yamaha. To the confusion of the experts and against their predictions Roberts took the 1978 title after a season long battle with Sheene. He repeated this in 1979 when Sheene demonstrated his great ability at Silverstone by pulling back after being baulked and running round Roberts at Woodcote to close to a wheel adrift at the line.

In 1980 Roberts made it three in a row with Randy Mamola runner up on the Suzuki and then in 1981 Lucchinelli brought the title back to Suzuki and the firm took the manufacturers title for the sixth time in a row. Uncini made it seven when he took the crown in 1982 but by then the RG500 was becoming old despite a revamp to the engine and a sophisticated rising rate rear suspension.

The 500 was now nine years on from its conception and so in 1983 had to give best to the Yamaha of Roberts and the Honda three of new champion Freddie Spencer. For all that the RG500 had a proud record over the years with its four rider and seven maker titles.

The broad success of the RG500 was shown from its early days when it dominated the 500 cc class lists and the spin-off cropped up in odd machines such as the TR100, TR125 and RJ100, the last built just to race in Indonesia.

One of the happiest victories for the Suzuki team was in the Senior TT in 1979 when the great Mike Hailwood won his last TT on a year old factory machine and a few days later so nearly won the Classic as well.

Thus by 1982, two decades after their first classic victory Suzuki could look to 13 riders titles and 15 maker's, a total of 28 world championships and every one gained with a simple but complex 2-stroke engine.

For more details of works road racing Suzuki machines and the riders who used them the reader is advised to turn to *Team Suzuki* written by Ray Battersby and published by Osprey Publishing.

Appendix

Specifications

Model	Power Free	Diamond Free	CO	COX
Year	**1952–54**	**1953–54**	**1954–55**	**1955**
No. cylinders	1	1	1	1
Bore (mm)	36	43	48	56
Stroke (mm)	36	40	50	50
Capacity (cc)	6·66 **1**	58	90·5	123
Compression ratio (to 1)		7·0		7·0
Power: bhp	1·0	2·0	4·0	4·0
@ rpm	4000	4000	5000	4000
Valve type	piston	piston	sv	sv
No. gears	1 **2**	2	3	3
Tyre (in.)	1·375 × 24	1·375 × 24	2·70 × 24	2·75 × 24
Front brake type	rim	nil	drum	drum
Rear brake type	rim	drum	drum	drum
Front suspension	nil	teles	teles	teles
Rear suspension	nil	nil	plunger	plunger
Dry weight (lb)		104	188	

1 later 50 cc   **2** later 2

Model	MF1	Porter Free	ST	TT1
Year	**1954–58**	**1955–57**	**1955–59**	**1956–59**
No. cylinders	1	1	1	2
Bore (mm)	38	52	52	54
Stroke (mm)	44	48	58	54
Capacity (cc)	49·9	101·9	123	247
Compression ratio (to 1)		7·0	7·0	
Power: bhp	2·0	4·2	5·5 **2**	16 **3**
@ rpm	4500	5000	5000 **2**	6000
Valve type	piston	piston	piston	piston
No. gears	belt	3	3	4
Tyre (in.)	1·375 × 24		2·75 × 24	3·25 × 16 **4**
Front brake type	rim	drum	drum	drum
Rear brake type	drum	drum	drum	drum
Front suspension	rigid	teles	teles	Earles **5**
Rear suspension	rigid	rigid	rigid **6**	s/a **7**
Dry weight (lb)		187		

1 1957—TP, 1958—TM   **2** 1956—6·5/5500, 1957—7/5500, 1958—7·5/5500, 1959—8/6000   **3** 1957—18
4 1958—3·00 × 18   **5** 1957—teles   **6** from 1955 also plunger, 1958 s/a   **7** 1958—plunger

Suzuki Two-strokes

Model	SM	SB to SL	MA	TA 1
Year	1958–59	1959–63	1960–62	1960–63
No. cylinders	1	2	1	2
Bore (mm)	38	42	41	52
Stroke (mm)	44	45	38	58
Capacity (cc)	49·9	125 **2**	50	246
Compression ratio (to 1)	7·1	7·0	6·1 **3**	6·3
Power: bhp	2·0 **4**	10 **5**	4	18 **6**
@ rpm	4500 **4**	8000 **5**	8000	7000 **6**
Valve type	piston		piston	piston
No. gears	belt **7**	4	4	4
Top gear ratio				6·8
Tyre (in.)	2·00 × 24	2·75 × 17 **8**	2·25 × 17	3·25 × 16 **9**
Brake type	drum	drum	drum	7 in drum
Front suspension	leading link	teles	leading link	teles
Rear suspension	s/a	s/a	s/a	s/a
Petrol tank (litre)				10
Ignition system				coil

1 1962—TB, 1963—TC **2** also 150 cc **3** 1962—6·7 **4** 1959—2·2/5000
5 1962—11·5, 1962 SL model—8/6000 **6** 1962—20/8000 **7** 1959—chain
8 1962—3·00 × 16 **9** 1962—3·00 × 17

Model	M15 1	M12	M30	U50 2
Year	1963–67	1963–67	1963–65	1966–68
No. cylinders	1	1	1	1
Bore (mm)	41	41	41	41
Stroke (mm)	38	38	38	37·8
Capacity (cc)	50	50	50	49·9
Compression ratio (to 1)	6·7	6·7	6·3	6·7
Valve type	piston	piston	piston	disc
bhp	4·2	4·2	4·0	4·1
@ rpm	8000	8000	6800	6000
Torque (Kg-m)	0·38		0·45	0·54
@ rpm	7000		5000	5000
Starting system	kick **3**	kick	kick	kick **3**
Oil system	mix	mix	mix	pump
Ignition timing degree	27		20	20
Ignition timing (mm)			1·4	1·4
Primary drive gearing	15/66	15/66	19/73	19/73
Final drive gearing	13/32	13/32	12/32	14/32
Box gearing: top	1·043	1·043	1·11	1·43
Box gearing: 3rd	1·431	1·431		
Box gearing: 2nd	1·939	1·939	1·64	2·11
Box gearing: 1st	3·167	3·167	2·93	4·18
O/A top gear ratio	11·30	11·30	11·37	12·60
No. gears	4	4	3	3

164

Specifications

Model	M15 **1**	M12	M30	U50 **2**
Year	**1963–67**	**1963–65**	**1963–65**	**1966–68**
Fuel (l)	6	6	3·5	3·4
Engine oil (l)				1·2
Box oil (l)	0·55		0·67	0·55
Tyres	2·25 × 17	2·25 × 17	2·25 × 17	2·25 × 17
Brakes	100 drum	100 drum	drum	drum
Front suspension	leading link	teles	leading link	leading link
Rear suspension	s/a	s/a	s/a	s/a
Ignition system	magneto **4**	magneto	magneto	magneto **4**
Wheelbase (in.)	45		44·5	46·5
Ground clear. (in.)	4·7		5·1	5·3
Width (in.)	23·6		24	24·2
Length (in.)	69·4		70·3	70·9
Dry weight (lb)	128 **5**	132	123	154 **6**

1 M15D also   **2** U50D also   **3** D model—elec. also   **4** D model—coil   **5** M15D–133   **6** U50D–153

Model	A50	AS50	AC50	A50P
Year	**1969–76**	**1968–70**	**1969–76**	**1975–77**
No. cylinders	1	1	1	1
Bore (mm)	41	41	41	41
Stroke (mm)	37·8	37·8	37·8	37·8
Capacity (cc)	49·9	49·9	49·9	49·9
Compression ratio (to 1)	6·7	6·7	6·7	6·7
Valve type	disc	disc	disc	disc **1**
bhp	4·9	4·9	4·9	4·8
@ rpm	8500	8500	8500	8500
Torque (Kg-m)	0·43	0·43	0·43	0·42
@ rpm	8000	8000	8000	8000
Starting system	kick	kick	kick	kick
Oil system	pump	pump	pump	pump **2**
Ignition timing degree	24	24	24	18
Ignition timing (mm)	2·01	2·01	2·01	1·14
Primary drive gearing	19/73	19/73	19/73	19/73
Final drive gearing	12/32 **3**	12/32	14/37	14/37
Box gearing: top	1·07	1·07	1·07	1·07
Box gearing: 4th	1·28	1·28	1·28	1·28
Box gearing: 3rd	1·59 **4**	1·59	1·59	1·59
Box gearing: 2nd	2·17 **5**	2·17	2·17	2·13
Box gearing: 1st	3·75 **6**	3·75	3·75 **6**	3·67
O/A top gear ratio	10·98 **7**	10·98	10·88	10·88
No. gears	5	5	5	5 **8**

Suzuki Two-strokes

Model	A50	AS50	AC50	A50P
Year	1969—76	1968—70	1969—76	1975—77
Fuel (l)	6·5 **9**	6·5	5·5	7·5
Engine oil (l)	1·4 **10**	1·4	1·2	1·2
Box oil (l)	0·55	0·55	0·55	0·55
Front fork/leg (cc)	125 **11**	125	125 **12**	138
Front tyre	2·25 × 17	2·25 × 17	2·25 × 17	2·25 × 17
Rear tyre	2·25 × 17	2·25 × 17	2·50 × 17 **13**	2·25 × 17 **14**
Front brake	110 drum	110 drum	110 drum	110 drum **15**
Rear brake	110 drum	110 drum	110 drum	110 drum
Front suspension	teles	teles	teles	teles
Rear suspension	s/a	s/a	s/a	s/a
Ignition system	magneto	magneto	magneto	magneto
Wheelbase (in.)	45·7 **16**	45·7	46·7	47·2
Ground clear. (in.)	5·9 **17**	5·9	5·9 **17**	4·9
Width (in.)	24·8 **18**	24·8	29·98 **18**	30·1
Length (in.)	70·3 **19**	70·3	71·5 **19**	71·7
Dry weight (lb)	158 **20**	160	160	165

1 reed—some countries   **2** mix—some countries   **3** 1971—14/37   **4** 1974—1·58   **5** 1974—2·13
6 1972—3·67   **7** 1971—10·88   **8** 4—some countries   **9** 1972—5·5   **10** 1972—1·2, 1974—1·0
11 1972—133, 1974—138   **12** 1972—138   **13** 1974—2·25 × 17   **14** some—2·50 × 17   **15** A50PD—disc
16 1971—46·7   **17** 1971—4·9   **18** 1971—31·1   **19** 1971—71·7   **20** 1971—160

Model	K50	F50 **1**	TS50	MT50
Year	1967–76	1969–76	1971–76	1971–73
No. cylinders	1	1	1	1
Bore (mm)	41	41	41	41
Stroke (mm)	37·8	37·8	37·8	37·8
Capacity (cc)	49·9	49·9	49·9	49·9
Compression ratio (to 1)	7·0 **2**	6·9	6·7	6·9
Valve type	reed	reed	disc	reed
bhp	4·2 **3**	4·5	4·9	3·8
@ rpm	8000 **3**	6000	8000	6000
Torque (Kg-m)	0·38 **4**	0·58	0·46	0·38
@ rpm	7000 **4**	5000	7000	5000
Starting system	kick	kick	kick	kick
Oil system	pump	pump	pump	pump
Ignition timing degree	20	20	24	20
Ignition timing (mm)	1·40	1·40	2·00	1·40
Primary drive gearing	15/66 **5**	19/73 **6**	19/73	19/73
Final drive gearing	13/32 **7**	13/32 **8**	15/42	13/28
Box gearing: top	1·04 **9**	1·45	1·07	1·45
Box gearing: 4th			1·28	
Box gearing: 3rd	1·43		1·58	
Box gearing: 2nd	1·94 **9**	2·20 **10**	2·13	2·20
Box gearing: 1st	3·17 **9**	4·18	3·67 **6**	4·18
O/A top gear ratio	11·26 **11**	13·71 **12**	11·52	12·00
No. gears	4 **13**	3	5	3

Specifications

Model	K50	F50 [1]	TS50	MT50
Year	1967–76	1969–76	1971–76	1971–73
Fuel (l)	6	3·2 [14]	5 [15]	2·5
Engine oil (l)	1·3 [16]	0·8 [17]	1·2	0·8
Box oil (l)	0·55 [18]	0·45 [19]	0·7	0·55
Front fork/leg (cc)	125 [20]		122 [21]	
Front tyre	2·25 × 17	2·25 × 17	2·25 × 17 [22]	3·50 × 8
Rear tyre	2·25 × 17	2·25 × 17	2·50 × 17	3·50 × 8
Brake	110 drum	110 drum	drum	drum
Front suspension	teles	leading link	teles	teles
Rear suspension	s/a	s/a	s/a	s/a
Ignition system	magneto	magneto	magneto	magneto
Wheelbase (in.)	45·7 [23]	46·5	46·7	37·0
Ground clear. (in.)	5·1 [24]	5·5	7·5	5·1
Width (in.)	26·2 [25]	25·6	32·7	25·6
Length (in.)	70·3 [26]	71·5	70·9	51·5
Dry weight (lb)	154 [27]	154	156	132

1 1974—FR50   **2** 1971—6·9   **3** 1971—4·5/6000   **4** 1971—0·52/5000   **5** 1970—19/73   **6** 1972—21/71
7 1970—14/32, 1974—13/35   **8** 1972—13/36   **9** 1970—1·45, 2·20, 4·18; 1974—1·24, 1·58, 2·20
10 1974—10·0   **11** 1970—12·73, 1974—12·83   **12** 1972—13·58   **13** 1970—3   **14** 1974—4·0
15 1974—4·5   **16** 1970—1·2   **17** 1974—0·7   **18** 1970—0·5   **19** 1974—0·4   **20** 1974—138
21 1972—136, 1974—110   **22** 1972—2·50 × 17   **23** 1970—46·8   **24** 1970—5·3   **25** 1970—29·5
26 1970—71·5   **27** 1970—162

Model	RV50	U70	F70 [1]	A70
Year	1973–76	1966–68	1969–76	1966–72
No. cylinders	1	1	1	1
Bore (mm)	41	46	46	46
Stroke (mm)	37·8	42	42	42
Capacity (cc)	49·9	69·8	69·8	69·8
Compression ratio (to 1)		7·0	6·6	7·0
Valve type	reed	disc	reed	disc
bhp	4·0 [2]	6·5	6·2	7·5
@ rpm	6000	7000	6500	7500
Torque (Kg-m)	0·50 [3]	0·75	0·71 [4]	0·80
@ rpm	5000	5500	5000 [4]	6000
Starting system	kick	kick	kick	kick
Oil system	pump	pump	pump	pump
Ignition timing degree	20	20	20 [5]	20
Ignition timing (mm)	1·42	1·56	1·56 [5]	1·56
Primary drive gearing	19/73	22/70	22/70	19/73
Final drive gearing	15/32	14/32	14/32 [6]	13/32 [7]
Box gearing: top	1·24	1·43	1·43	1·07
Box gearing: 3rd	1·58			1·48
Box gearing: 2nd	2·20	2·11	2·11	2·05
Box gearing: 1st	3·67	3·38	3·38	3·31
O/A top gear ratio	10·16	10·43	10·43 [8]	10·12 [9]
No. gears	4	3	3	4

167

Suzuki Two-strokes

Model	RV50	U70	F70	A70
Year	1973–76	1966–68	1969–76	1966–72
Fuel (l)	3·5	3·4	3·2 **10**	6
Engine oil (l)	0·7	1·2	0·8 **11**	1·2
Box oil (l)	0·5	0·55	0·55	0·55
Front fork/leg (cc)	100			125 **12**
Front tyre	5·40 × 10	2·25 × 17	2·25 × 17	2·25 × 17
Rear tyre	5·40 × 10	2·25 × 17	2·25 × 17	2·50 × 17
Brake	drum	110 drum	110 drum	110 drum
Front suspension	teles	leading link	leading link	teles
Rear suspension	s/a	s/a	s/a	s/a
Ignition system	magneto	magneto	magneto	magneto
Wheelbase (in.)		46·5	46·5	45·6 **13**
Ground clear. (in.)	5·5 **14**	5·3	5·3 **15**	5·9 **16**
Width (in.)	30·5	24·2	25·6	26·5 **17**
Length (in.)	64·6 **18**	70·9	71·5 **19**	71·5
Dry weight (lb)	165	159	156 **20**	162 **21**

1 1974—FR70   **2** 1975—3·9   **3** 1975—0·49   **4** 1974—0·74/4500   **5** 1974—18/1·29   **6** 1974—14/36
7 1971—14/35   **8** 1974—11·74   **9** 1971—10·28   **10** 1974—4·0   **11** 1974—0·7   **12** 1972—138
13 1971—46·7   **14** 1976—4·9   **15** 1974—5·1   **16** 1971—5·1   **17** 1971—29·9   **18** 1976—63·9
19 1974—71·9   **20** 1974—176   **21** 1971—165

Model	TS75	TM75	RV75	A80
Year	1974–77	1973–76	1974–76	1972–76
No. cylinders	1	1	1	1
Bore (mm)	47	47	47	47
Stroke (mm)	42	42	42	42
Capacity (cc)	72·9	72·9	72·9	72·9
Compression ratio (to 1)		6·8		7·0
Valve type	disc	disc	disc	disc
bhp		5·0	6·5	7·7
@ rpm		6500	6000	7500
Torque (Kg-m)		0·58	0·83	0·83
@ rpm		6000	5000	6000
Starting system	kick	kick	kick	kick
Oil system	pump	pump	pump	pump
Ignition timing degree	20	20		20
Ignition timing (mm)	1·56	1·56		1·56
Primary drive gearing	19/73	19/73		19/73
Final drive gearing	15/42	15/42		14/35
Box gearing: top	1·11	1·07		1·07
Box gearing: 3rd	1·48	1·48		1·48
Box gearing: 2nd	2·05	2·05		2·05
Box gearing: 1st	3·31	3·31		3·31
O/A top gear ratio	11·94	11·51		10·28
No. gears	4	4	4	4

Specifications

Model	TS75	TM75	RV75	A80
Year	1974–77	1973–76	1974–76	1972–76
Fuel (l)	4·5	4·5	3·5	7·0
Engine oil (l)	1·2	1·2		1·3
Box oil (l)	0·7	0·7		0·55
Front fork/leg (cc)	110	100		138
Front tyre	2·50 × 16	2·50 × 16	5·40 × 10	2·25 × 17
Rear tyre	3·00 × 14	3·00 × 14	5·40 × 10	2·50 × 17
Brake	drum	drum	drum	110 drum
Front suspension	teles	teles	teles	teles
Rear suspension	s/a	s/a	s/a	s/a
Ignition system	magneto	magneto	magneto	magneto
Wheelbase (in.)		46·9		46·7
Ground clear. (in.)		6·3	4·9	5·1
Width (in.)		30·7	30·5	29·9
Length (in.)		69·3	63·9	71·5
Dry weight (lb)		165	183	165

Model	K10 1	K11 2	TC90	TS90
Year	1962–68	1963–69	1970–72	1970–72
No. cylinders	1	1	1	1
Bore (mm)	45	45	47	47
Stroke (mm)	50	50	51·8	51·8
Capacity (cc)	79·5	79·5	89·9	89·9
Compression ratio (to 1)	6·7	6·7	6·8	6·8
Valve type	piston	piston	disc	disc
bhp	7·5	8·0	11	11
@ rpm	6500	7500	7500	7500
Torque (Kg-m)	0·89	0·86	1·08	1·08
@ rpm	5000	6000	7000	7000
Starting system	kick	kick	kick	kick
Oil system	mix 3	mix 3	pump	pump
Ignition timing degree	27	27	20	20
Ignition timing (mm)			1·96	1·96
Primary drive gearing	19/73	19/73	23/73	23/73
Final drive gearing	13/30 4	14/30	14/47	14/51
Box gearing: top	1·07	1·07	0·95 1·64	0·87
Box gearing: 4th				1·10
Box gearing: 3rd	1·47	1·47	1·21 2·10	1·39
Box gearing: 2nd	2·03	2·03	1·64 2·85	1·87
Box gearing: 1st	3·35	3·35	2·50 4·34	2·82
O/A top gear ratio	9·487 5	8·809	10·09	10·05
No. gears	4	4	4 × 2	5

169

Suzuki Two-strokes

Model	K10 [1]	K11 [2]	TC90	TS90
Year	1962–68	1963–69	1970–72	1970–72
Fuel (l)	7 [6]	7 [6]	6 [7]	6 [7]
Engine oil (l)	1·3 [8]	1·3 [8]	1·2	1·2
Box oil (l)	0·65	0·65	0·8 [9]	0·8 [9]
Front fork/leg (cc)			185	185
Front tyre	2·50 × 17	2·50 × 17	2·75 × 18	2·75 × 18
Rear tyre	2·50 × 17	2·50 × 17	3·00 × 18	2·75 × 18 [10]
Brake	110 drum	110 drum	140 drum	140 drum
Front suspension	teles	teles	teles	teles
Rear suspension	s/a	s/a	s/a	s/a
Ignition system	magneto	magneto	magneto	magneto
Wheelbase (in.)	45·7	45·7	45·7 [11]	47·7 [11]
Ground clear. (in.)	5·1	5·3	8·9 [12]	8·7 [13]
Width (in.)	24·1	24·1	32·6 [14]	32·6 [14]
Length (in.)	70·3	72·1 [15]	74·8 [16]	72·3 [17]
Dry weight (lb)	155 [18]	155 [18]	199 [19]	197

[1] 1967—K10P   [2] 1967—K11P   [3] 1967—pump   [4] 1967—14/30   [5] 1967—8·809   [6] 1967—6
[7] 1972—6·5   [8] 1967 on   [9] 1971—0·7   [10] 1971—3·00 × 18   [11] 1971—47·4, 1972—47·0
[12] 1971—9·0, 1972—8·7   [13] 1971—8·9, 1972—6·8   [14] 1972—33·1   [15] 1967—71·6
[16] 1971—75·2, 1972—73·8   [17] 1971—74·6, 1972—73·8   [18] 1967—167   [19] 1972—198

Model	RV90	A100	ACC100	ASS100
Year	1971–76	1967–80	1970–71	1970–71
No. cylinders	1	1	1	1
Bore (mm)	50	50	50	50
Stroke (mm)	45	50	50	50
Capacity (cc)	88·4	98·2	98·2	98·2
Compression ratio (to 1)	6·2	6·5	6·5	6·5
Valve type	reed	disc	disc	disc
bhp	8·0 [1]	9·5	10·0	9·5
@ rpm	6000	7500	8000	7500
Torque (Kg-m)	1·0 [2]	0·95	0·94	0·95
@ rpm	4000	6500	7000	6500
Starting system	kick	kick	kick	kick
Oil system	pump	pump	pump	pump
Ignition timing degree	22	20	20	20
Ignition timing (mm)	2·04	1·86	1·86	1·86
Primary drive gearing	15/52	16/50	16/50	16/50
Final drive gearing	15/47	13/32 [3]	13/35	13/34
Box gearing: top	1·10	1·10	1·10	1·10
Box gearing: 3rd	1·47	1·39	1·39	1·39
Box gearing: 2nd	1·87	1·87	1·87	1·87
Box gearing: 1st	2·91	2·91	2·91	2·91
O/A top gear ratio	11·95	8·462 [4]	9·255	8·990
No. gears	4	4	4	4

170

Model	RV90	A100	ACC100	ASS100
Year	1971–76	1967–80	1970–71	1970–71
Fuel (l)	4·3	7·0 **5**	7·0	6·5
Engine oil (l)	0·8	1·2	1·4	1·4
Box oil (l)	0·7	0·75 **6**	0·7	0·65
Front fork/leg (cc)	98	125	125	125
Front tyre	6·70 × 10	2·50 × 17 **7**	2·50 × 18	2·50 × 18
Rear tyre	6·70 × 10	2·50 × 17 **7**	2·75 × 18	2·50 18
Brake	drum	140 drum	drum	drum
Front suspension	teles	teles	teles	teles
Rear suspension	s/a	s/a	s/a	s/a
Ignition system	magneto	magneto	magneto	magneto
Wheelbase (in.)	46·5	45·6 **8**	46·9	46·9
Ground clear. (in.)	7·7	5·3 **9**	8·1	6·1
Width (in.)	32·3	26·7 **10**	30·7	26·7
Length (in.)	71·1	71·6 **11**	72·4	72·4
Dry weight (lb)	185	176 **12**	184	180

1 1976—7·8 **2** 1976—0·98 **3** 1971—13/34, 1972—14/37 **4** 1971—8·990, 1972—9·085
5 1971—6·5, 1972—6·0, 1973—7·0 **6** 1973—0·65 **7** 1971—2·50 × 18 **8** 1971—46·9, 1972—47·2
9 1971—6·1, 1972—5·5 **10** 1972—29·9 **11** 1971—72·4, 1972—72·0 **12** 1971—180, 1972—183

Model	TC100	TS100	TM100	GT100
Year	1973–76	1973–77	1974–75	1975–76
No. cylinders	1	1	1	1
Bore (mm)	49	49		49
Stroke (mm)	51·8	51·8		51·4
Capacity (cc)	97·7	97·7		96·9
Compression ratio (to 1)	6·5	6·5		
Valve type	disc	disc	disc	disc
bhp	11	11	16·5	12
@ rpm	7000	7000	10000	8000
Torque (Kg-m)	1·19	1·19	1·18	1·1
@ rpm	6000	6000	9000	7500
Starting system	kick	kick	kick	kick
Oil system	pump	pump	pump	pump
Ignition timing degree	20	20		
Ignition timing (mm)	2·22	2·22		
Primary drive gearing	23/73	23/73	17/57	23/73
Final drive gearing	13/47	13/49	14/64	14/46
Box gearing: top	0·95 1·54	0·87	0·91	0·87
Box gearing: 4th		1·10	1·04	1·10
Box gearing: 3rd	1·21 1·97	1·39	1·25	1·39
Box gearing: 2nd	1·64 2·67	1·87	1·59	1·87
Box gearing: 1st	2·50 4·06	2·82	2·14	2·82
O/A top gear ratio	10·87	10·40	13·99	9·068
No. gears	4 × 2	5	5	5

Specifications

Suzuki Two-strokes

Model	TC100	TS100	TM100	GT100
Year	1973–76	1973–77	1974–75	1975–76
Fuel (l)	6·5	6·5	5·0	10
Engine oil (l)	1·1	1·1	0·55	
Box oil (l)	0·7	0·7	0·55	
Front fork/leg (cc)	125	125	123	
Front tyre	2·75 × 19	2·75 × 19	3·00 × 21	2·50 × 18
Rear tyre	3·00 × 18	3·00 × 18	3·50 × 18	2·75 × 18
Front brake	110 drum	110 drum	drum	disc
Rear brake	110 drum	110 drum	drum	110 drum
Front suspension	teles	teles	teles	teles
Rear suspension	s/a	s/a	s/a	s/a
Ignition system	magneto	magneto		PEI
Wheelbase (in.)	49·2	49·2		48·2
Ground clear. (in.)	7·7	7·7		5·1
Width (in.)	32·7	32·7		30·3
Length (in.)	78·7	78·7		74·8
Dry weight (lb)	205	202		207

Model	B100 1	KT120 2	B120 3	K125
Year	1964–70	1967–72	1967–77	1967–76
No. cylinders	1	1	1	1
Bore (mm)	52	52	52	54
Stroke (mm)	56	56	56	54
Capacity (cc)	119	119	119	124
Compression ratio (to 1)	6·8	7·2 4	6·8	7·0
Valve type	piston	piston	piston	disc
bhp	10	9·5 5	10	10·5
@ rpm	7000	6500 5	7000	7000
Torque (kg-m)	1·1	1·23 6	1·1	1·17
@ rpm	5000	5000 6	5000	5500
Starting system	kick	kick	kick	kick
Oil system	mix 7	pump	pump	pump
Ignition timing degree	24	24	24	15 8
Ignition timing (mm)	3·00	3·00	3·00	1·12 8
Primary drive gearing	16/50	16/50	16/50	17/64
Final drive gearing	14/31	13/35 9	14/31	15/38
Box gearing: top	1·10	1·05 2·07	1·10	0·88
Box gearing: 3rd	1·39		1·39	1·14
Box gearing: 2nd	1·87	1·39 2·75	1·87	1·56
Box gearing: 1st	2·91	2·23 4·41	2·91	2·54
O/A top gear ratio	7·612	8·814 10	7·612	8·393
No. gears	4	3 × 2	4	4

Specifications

Model	B100 **1**	KT120 **2**	B120 **3**	K125
Year	1964–70	1967–72	1967–77	1967–76
Fuel (l)	8	8 **11**	8	10 **12**
Engine oil (l)	1·3	1·3 **13**	1·3	1·5
Box oil (l)	0·8	0·8	0·8	0·8
Front fork/leg (cc)	160	160 **14**	160	180
Front tyre	2·50 × 17	2·75 × 17 **15**	2·50 × 17	3·00 × 16
Rear tyre	2·75 × 17	3·00 × 17 **15**	2·75 × 17	3·00 × 16
Brake	150 drum	drum **16**	140 drum	drum
Front suspension	teles	teles	teles	teles
Rear suspension	s/a	s/a	s/a	s/a
Ignition system	magneto	magneto	magneto	coil
Wheelbase (in.)	48	48 **17**	48	49·6
Ground clear. (in.)	5·9	6·5 **18**	5·9	4·9
Width (in.)	26·2	29·3 **19**	26·2	27·6 **20**
Length (in.)	74·9	75·7 **21**	74·9	74·8 **22**
Dry weight (lb)	189	201 **23**	187	248

1 1966—B100P **2** 1969—TC120 **3** 1975—B120S **4** 1969—6·9 **5** 1969—12/7500 **6** 1969—1·2/7000
7 1966—Pump **8** 1971—20/1·99 **9** 1969—14/41 **10** 1969—9·660 **11** 1969—7 **12** 1971—9
13 1969—1·4 **14** 1969—175 **15** 1969—18 in. **16** 1969—140 Drum **17** 1969—47
18 1969—7·9 **19** 1969—31·3 **20** 1971—30·7 **21** 1969—73·4 **22** 1971—75 **23** 1969—209, 1971—205

Model	TC125	TS125	TM125	RV125
Year	1972–76	1971–77	1973–75	1973–77
No. cylinders	1	1	1	1
Bore (mm)	56	56	56	56
Stroke (mm)	50	50	50	50
Capacity (cc)	123	123	123	123
Compression ratio (to 1)	6·7	6·7	7·5	6·3
Valve type	piston	piston	piston	piston
bhp	13·0 **1**	13·0 **1**	20 **2**	10
@ rpm	7000	7000	10000	6000
Torque (Kg-m)	1·36 **3**	1·36 **3**	1·44 **4**	1·22
@ rpm	6500 **3**	6500 **3**	9500 **4**	5500
Starting system	kick	kick	kick	kick
Oil system	pump	pump	pump	pump
Ignition timing degree	22	22	29 **5**	22
Ignition timing (mm)	2·41	2·41		2·41
Primary drive gearing	16/57	16/57	16/57 **6**	16/57
Final drive gearing	12/37	15/50	15/61 **7**	15/51
Box gearing: top	0·86 1·57	0·80	0·91	0·80
Box gearing: 4th		1·00	1·05	1·00
Box gearing: 3rd	1·11 2·01	1·25	1·25	1·25
Box gearing: 2nd	1·56 2·84	1·81	1·59	1·81
Box gearing: 1st	2·46 4·47	2·75	2·14	2·75
O/A top gear ratio	9·486	9·500	13·23 **8**	9·690
No. gears	4 × 2	5	5	5

Suzuki Two-strokes

Model	TC125	TS125	TM125	RV125
Year	1972–76	1971–77	1973–75	1973–77
Fuel (l)	7·0	7·0	5·0	4·7
Engine oil (l)	1·1	1·1	0·55	0·8
Box oil (l)	0·55	0·55	0·55	0·55
Front fork/leg (cc)	195 **9**	195 **9**	130 **10**	125
Front tyre	2·75 × 19	2·75 × 19 **11**	3·00 × 21	5·40 × 14
Rear tyre	3·25 × 18	3·25 × 18	3·50 × 18	6·70 × 12
Front brake	115 drum	115 drum	110 drum	110 drum
Rear brake	140 drum	140 drum	110 drum	130 drum
Front suspension	teles	teles	teles	teles
Rear suspension	s/a	s/a	s/a	s/a
Ignition system	magneto	magneto	PEI	magneto
Wheelbase (in.)	51·6	51·6	52·6	51·4
Ground clear. (in.)	9·3	9·3	7·9	7·7
Width (in.)	33·3	33·3	36·8	30·3
Length (in.)	79·7	80·7	79·1	77·2
Dry weight (lb)	209	198	189	244

1 1975—12·7, 1976—14   **2** 18 with silencer   **3** 1975—1·33/6500, 1976—1·50/6000   **4** 1·38/8000 with silencer
5 at 6000   **6** 1974—17/57   **7** 1974—15/64   **8** 1974—13·06   **9** 1974—124   **10** 1974—123
11 1974—2·75 × 21

Model	TC185	TS185	TS250	TM250
Year	1974–76	1971–77	1969–77	1972–75
No. cylinders	1	1	1	1
Bore (mm)	64	64	70	70
Stroke (mm)	57	57	64	64
Capacity (cc)	183	183	246	246
Compression ratio (to 1)	6·2	6·2	6·62 **1**	7·5
Valve type	piston	piston	piston	piston
bhp	16	17·5	23	30
@ rpm	7000	7000	6500	7500
Torque (Kg-m)	1·8	1·86	2·71 **2**	2·90
@ rpm	5500	6000	5000 **2**	7000
Starting system	elec, kick	kick	kick	kick
Oil system	pump	pump	pump	pump
Ignition timing degree	24	24	21	21·5
Ignition timing (mm)	3·07	3·07	2·7	
Primary drive gearing	21/67	19/61	22/58 **3**	21/67 **4**
Final drive gearing	12/39	12/39	15/50 **5**	15/40 **6**
Box gearing: top	0·80 1·12	0·80	0·80 **7**	0·83 **8**
Box gearing: 4th	1·00 1·41	1·00	0·96	1·00
Box gearing: 3rd	1·25 1·76	1·25	1·19	1·28
Box gearing: 2nd	1·81 2·55	1·81	1·56	1·80
Box gearing: 1st	2·75 3·87	2·75	2·29	2·42
O/A top gear ratio	8·295	8·347	7·030 **9**	7·028 **10**
No. gears	5 × 2	5	5	5

Specifications

Model	TC185	TS185	TS250	TM250
Year	**1974–76**	**1971–77**	**1969–77**	**1972–75**
Fuel (l)	7·0	7·0	8·9 **11**	9·0
Engine oil (l)	1·1	1·1	1·5 **12**	0·6
Box oil (l)	0·75	0·55	1·1 **13**	0·7 **14**
Front fork/leg (cc)	124	195 **15**	250 **16**	190 **17**
Front tyre	3·00 × 19	3·00 × 19 **18**	3·25 × 19 **18**	3·00 × 21
Rear tyre	3·50 × 18	3·50 × 18	4·00 × 18	4·00 × 18
Front brake	110 drum	110 drum	150 drum	150 drum
Rear brake	110 drum	130 drum	150 drum	180 drum
Front suspension	teles	teles	teles	teles
Rear suspension	s/a	s/a	s/a	s/a
Ignition system	coil	magneto **19**	magneto **19**	PEI
Wheelbase (in.)	52·6	52·8 **20**	53·9 **21**	55·8
Ground clear. (in.)	9·4	9·4	9·5 **22**	8·5
Width (in.)	33·3	33·0 **23**	32·5 **24**	34·3
Length (in.)	79·1	79·5 **25**	83·3 **26**	84·5
Dry weight (lb)	271	217	280 **27**	220

1 1972—6·7 **2** 1972—2·68/5500 **3** 1972—21/67 **4** 1974—23/71 **5** 1972—15/39, 1974—15/40
6 1974—15/45 **7** 1972—0·83, 1·0, 1·28, 1·80, 2·42 **8** 1974—0·86, 1·05, 1·28, 1·56, 1·93
9 1972—6·853, 1974—7·028 **10** 1974—7·998 **11** 1971—9·0 **12** 1971—1·05, 1974—1·1
13 1971—1·2, 1972—0·7, 1974—0·85 **14** 1974—0·85 **15** 1974—124 **16** 1971—255, 1974—180
17 1974—187 **18** 1974—2·75 × 21 **19** 1972—PEI **20** 1975—52·5 **21** 1971—55·8 **22** 1971—9·8
23 1975—31·0 **24** 1971—34·3 **25** 1975—82·0 **26** 1971—86·0 **27** 1971—273, 1972—260

Model	RL250	RL325	TM400	TS400
Year	**1973–80**	**1978–80**	**1971–75**	**1972–76**
No. cylinders	1	1	1	1
Bore (mm)	70	80	82	82
Stroke (mm)	64	64	75	75
Capacity (cc)	246	322	396	396
Compression ratio (to 1)	6·7	7·5	7·3	6·8 **1**
Valve type	piston **2**	reed	piston	piston
bhp	18 **3**	23	40 **4**	34 **5**
@ rpm	6000	6500	6500	6000
Torque (Kg-m)	2·3		4·53 **6**	4·11 **7**
@ rpm	4500		6000 **6**	5500
Starting system	kick	kick	kick	kick
Oil system	mix	mix	pump	pump
Ignition timing degree	21 **8**		19·5	22
Primary drive gearing	18/75 **9**	22/58	23/68	23/68
Final drive gearing	15/54	12/39	15/40	16/40
Box gearing: top	0·64	0·80	0·84	0·84 **10**
Box gearing: 4th	0·86	0·96	0·96	0·96
Box gearing: 3rd	1·41	1·19	1·14	1·14
Box gearing: 2nd	1·80	1·56	1·42	1·42
Box gearing: 1st	2·42	2·29	1·88	2·07
O/A top gear ratio	9·600 **11**	6·854	6·623	6·209 **12**
No. gears	5	5	5	5

Suzuki Two-strokes

Model	RL250	RL325	TM400	TS400
Year	1973–80	1978–80	1971–75	1972–76
Fuel (l)	5·0 **13**	4·1	9·0 **14**	9·0
Engine oil (l)			0·4 **15**	1·2
Box oil (l)	0·7 **16**	0·8	1·1 **17**	1·2
Front fork/leg (cc)	236 **18**	195	190 **19**	255 **20**
Front tyre	2·75 × 21	2·75 × 21	3·00 × 21	3·25 × 19 **21**
Rear tyre	4·00 × 18	4·00 × 18	4·00 × 18	4·00 × 18
Brake	drum	drum	drum	160 drum
Front suspension	teles	teles	teles	teles
Rear suspension	s/a	s/a	s/a	s/a
Ignition system	PEI	PEI	PEI	PEI
Wheelbase (in.)	53·0 **22**	52·0	55·5	54·6
Ground clear. (in.)	11·4 **23**	13·0	8·7	8·0 **24**
Width (in.)	33·5	33·0	34·4	35·0 **25**
Length (in.)	80·1	79·9	85·0	87·2 **26**
Dry weight (lb)	199 **27**	201	231	277

1 1975—7·3 **2** later with reed **3** 1980—19 **4** 1975—35 **5** 1975—33 **6** 1975—4·3/5500
7 1975—3·99 **8** at 4000 **9** 1974—17/72 **10** 1974—0·81, 0·96, 1·14, 1·42, 2·29 **11** 1974—9·758, 1977—9·0
12 1974—5·970 **13** 1980—4·1 **14** 1974—8·0 **15** 1972—0·7, 1974—0·55 **16** 1974—0·85 **17** 1972—1·2
18 1974—245 **19** 1974—187 **20** 1974—180 **21** 1974—3·00 × 21 **22** 1980—52 **23** 1980—13
24 1975—8·5 **25** 1975—32·7 **26** 1975—86·2 **27** 1977—194, 1979—188, 1980—200

Model	S30/S31	T125	GT125	S32
Year	1963–67	1969–73	1974–79	1963–67
No. cylinders	2	2	2	2
Bore (mm)	42	43	43	46
Stroke (mm)	45	43	43	45
Capacity (cc)	124·7	124·9	124·9	149·6
Compression ratio (to 1)	7·0	7·3	6·8	7·4
Valve type	piston	piston	piston	piston
bhp	11 **1**	15·1	16	12
@ rpm	7000 **1**	8500	9500	7000
Torque (Kg-m)	1·20	1·38	1·3	1·25
@ rpm	6000 **2**	7000	9000	6000
Starting system	elec, kick	kick	kick	elec, kick
Oil system	mix	pump	pump	mix
Ignition timing degree	25	24 **3**	22	25
Ignition timing (mm)	2·48	2·28	1·93 **4**	2·48
Primary drive gearing	17/62	16/50	19/61	20/59
Final drive gearing	14/38	16/40	14/50	13/38
Box gearing: top	0·88	1·09	0·80 **5**	0·92
Box gearing: 4th		1·24	0·96 **6**	
Box gearing: 3rd	1·14	1·56	1·25	1·14
Box gearing: 2nd	1·56	2·07	1·81	1·56
Box gearing: 1st	2·54	3·18	3·00	2·54
O/A top gear ratio	8·711	8·523	9·173 **7**	7·933
No. gears	4	5	5	4

Model	S30/S31	T125	GT125	S32
Year	**1963–67**	**1969–73**	**1974–79**	**1963–67**
Fuel (l)	8	8	10	8
Engine oil (l)		1·4	1·2	
Box oil (l)	1·2	0·85	0·9	1·2
Front fork/leg (cc)	180	130	125	180
Front tyre	3·00 × 16	2·50 × 18	2·75 × 18	2·75 × 17
Rear tyre	3·00 × 16	2·75 × 18	3·00 × 18	2·75 × 17
Front brake	160 drum	140 drum	250 disc	160 drum
Rear brake	160 drum	140 drum	130 drum	160 drum
Front suspension	teles	teles	teles	teles
Rear suspension	s/a	s/a	s/a	s/a
Ignition system	coil	coil	coil	coil
Wheelbase (in.)	49·6	46·9	48·5	49·6
Ground clear. (in.)	5·1	6·7	5·7	5·1
Width (in.)	26·6	31·1	28·9	30·1
Length (in.)	76·0	72·2	75·4	74·8
Dry weight (lb)	243	211	238	253

1 S31—12/8000   **2** S31—7000   **3** 1970—20   **4** 1976—1·94   **5** 1976—0·88   **6** 1976—1·00
7 1976—10·03

Model	GT185	T200	T10	T20
Year	**1973–79**	**1967–70**	**1963–67**	**1966–68**
No. cylinders	2	2	2	2
Bore (mm)	49	50	52	54
Stroke (mm)	49	50	58	54
Capacity (cc)	184·8	196	246	247
Compression ratio (to 1)	7·0	7·0	6·3	7·3
Valve type	piston	piston	piston	piston
bhp	21 **1**	23	21	29
@ rpm	7500	7500	8000	7500
Torque (Kg-m)	2·10 **2**	2·30	2·10	2·82
@ rpm	6000	7000	7000	7000
Starting system	elec, kick	kick	elec, kick	kick
Oil system	pump	pump	mix	pump
Ignition timing degree	20	24	7 to 30	27
Ignition timing (mm)	1·83 **3**	2·68	0·27–4·76	3·62
Primary drive gearing	19/61	20/59	21/69	22/59
Final drive gearing	14/40	14/37	12/30	14/41
Box gearing: top	0·80	0·92	0·74	0·79
Box gearing: 5th				0·89
Box gearing: 4th	1·00	1·09		1·04
Box gearing: 3rd	1·25	1·32	0·96	1·27
Box gearing: 2nd	1·81	1·72	1·47	1·63
Box gearing: 1st	2·75	2·77	2·54	2·57
O/A top gear ratio	7·338	7·197	6·085	6·171
No. gears	5	5	4	6

Suzuki Two-strokes

Model	GT185	T200	T10	T20
Year	1973–79	1967–70	1963–67	1966–68
Fuel (l)	10	12	10	14
Engine oil (l)	1·2	1·6		2·2
Box oil (l)	0·8	1·0	0·5	1·2
Front fork/leg (cc)	125 **4**	180	230	200
Front tyre	2·75 × 18	2·75 × 18	3·00 × 17	2·75 × 18
Rear tyre	3·00 × 18	2·75 × 18	3·00 × 17	3·00 × 18
Front brake	160 drum **5**	160 drum	165 drum	200 drum
Rear brake	130 drum	150 drum	165 drum	200 drum
Front suspension	teles	teles	teles	teles
Rear suspension	s/a	s/a	s/a	s/a
Ignition system	coil	coil	coil	coil
Wheelbase (in.)	50·6	49·4	53·2	50·4
Ground clear. (in.)	6·5	5·7	5·3	6·5
Width (in.)	29·9	30·1	31·5	30·1
Length (in.)	78·0	75·8	81·4	76·8
Dry weight (lb)	253	269	330	298

1 1974—20 **2** 1974—2·04 **3** 1975—2·62, 1976—2·64 **4** 1974—130 **5** 1974—250 disc

Model	T250 **1**	T305	T350	T500 **2**
Year	1969–78	1968–69	1969–73	1967–77
No. cylinders	2	2	2	2
Bore (mm)	54	60	61	70
Stroke (mm)	54	54	54	64
Capacity (cc)	247	305	316	493
Compression ratio (to 1)	7·5 **3**	6·68	6·94	6·6
Valve type	piston	piston	piston	piston
bhp	32	37	39 **4**	46 **5**
@ rpm	8000	7500	7500 **4**	7000 **5**
Torque (Kg-m)	3·0 **6**	3·60	4·0 **7**	5·24 **8**
@ rpm	7000 **6**	7000	6500 **7**	5500 **8**
Starting system	kick	kick	kick	kick
Oil system	pump	pump	pump	pump
Ignition timing degree	24 **9**	24	24	24 **10**
Ignition timing (mm)	2·88 **9**	2·88	2·88	3·40 **10**
Primary drive gearing	20/61	20/61	20/61	26/65
Final drive gearing	14/41 **11**	14/38	14/38	14/33 **12**
Box gearing: top	0·71	0·70	0·71	0·87
Box gearing: 5th:	0·78	0·80	0·78	
Box gearing: 4th	0·90	0·95	0·90	0·95
Box gearing: 3rd	1·16 **13**	1·14	1·16	1·16
Box gearing: 2nd	1·50 **14**	1·50	1·50	1·56
Box gearing: 1st	2·33	2·33	2·33	2·50
O/A top gear ratio	6·327 **15**	5·826	5·864	5·124 **16**
No. gears	6	6	6	5

Specifications

Model	T250 **1**	T305	T350	T500 **2**
Year	**1969–78**	**1968–69**	**1969–73**	**1967–77**
Fuel (l)	12 **17**	14	12 **18**	14 **19**
Engine oil (l)	1·8 **20**	1·8	1·8 **21**	1·8
Box oil (l)	1·2 **22**	1·2	1·2	1·2 **23**
Front fork/leg (cc)	220 **24**	220	220	220 **25**
Front tyre	2·75 × 18 **26**	3·00 × 18	3·00 × 18	3·25 × 19
Rear tyre	3·00 × 18 **27**	3·25 × 18	3·25 × 18	4·00 × 18
Front brake	180 drum **28**	drum	180 drum	200 drum **29**
Rear brake	180 drum	drum	160 drum	180 drum
Front suspension	teles	teles	teles	teles
Rear suspension	s/a	s/a	s/a	s/a
Ignition system	coil	coil	coil	coil **30**
Wheelbase (in.)	50·8 **31**	50·8	50·8 **32**	56·1 **33**
Ground clear. (in.)	6·1 **34**	6·3	6·3	6·3
Width (in.)	32·3	32·5	32·5 **35**	32·9 **36**
Length (in.)	77·8 **37**	77·8	77·8 **38**	80·7 **39**
Dry weight (lb)	283 **40**	317	285 **41**	403 **42**

1 1973—GT250 **2** 1976—GT500 **3** 1976—7·3 **4** 1970—40/7500, 1971—36/7000 **5** 1969—47/7000, 1976—44/6000 **6** 1973—3·18/6500 **7** 1971—3·9/6000 **8** 1969—5·3/6000, 1976—5·4/5500 **9** 1976—20/2·05 **10** to 1975 **11** 1976—14/43 **12** 196915/33 **13** 1973—1·10, 1976—1·05 **14** 1976—1·35 **15** 1976—6·636 **16** 1969—4·783 **17** 1976—15 **18** 1971—15 **19** 1976—17 **20** 1976—1·1 **21** 1970—1·5, 1971—1·1 **22** 1975—1·3 **23** 1974—1·4 **24** 1975—145 **25** 1976—266 **26** 1973—3·00 × 18 **27** 1973—3·25 × 18 **28** 1973—275 disc **29** 1976—275 disc **30** 1976—CDI **31** 1973—57·5, 1976—51·6 **32** 1971—51·2 **33** 1969—57·2 **34** 1973—6·3 **35** 1970—34·6, 1971—34·3 **36** 1972—34·6 **37** 1973—80·5 **38** 1970—78·3, 1971—79·9 **39** 1969—85·5, 1972—86·4 **40** 1973—322 **41** 1971—339 **42** 1969—412, 1972—408, 1976—395

Model	GT380	GT550	GT550	RE5
Year	**1972–79**	**1972–77**	**1972–77**	**1974–77**
No. cylinders	3	3	3	1 rotor
Bore (mm)	54	61	70	
Stroke (mm)	54	62	64	
Capacity (cc)	371	544	739	497
Compression ratio (to 1)	6·7	6·8	6·7 **1**	8·6
Valve type	piston	piston	piston	ports
bhp	38 **2**	50 **3**	67 **4**	62
@ rpm	7500	6500 **3**	6500	6500
Torque (Kg-m)	3·93 **5**	6·1 **6**	7·7 **7**	7·6
@ rpm	6000	5000 **6**	5500	3500
Starting system	kick	elec, kick	elec, kick	elec, kick
Oil system	pump	pump	pump	pump
Ignition timing degree	24	24	24	10
Ignition timing (mm)	3·00 **8**	3·37 **9**	R, L—3·63 C—3·42 **10**	
Primary drive gearing	24/68	33/74	49/82	23/38
Final drive gearing	14/42	16/40 **11**	15/47 **12**	14/43
Box gearing: top	0·71	0·92 **13**	0·92 **14**	0·92

Suzuki Two-strokes

	GT380 1972–79	GT550 1972–77	GT550 1972–77	RE5 1974–77
Box gearing: 5th:	0.78			
Box gearing: 4th	0.90	1·12	1·12	1·12
Box gearing: 3rd	1·16	1·36	1·36 **15**	1·36
Box gearing: 2nd	1·50	1·74	1·74 **15**	1·74
Box gearing: 1st	2·33	2·85	2·85	2·85
O/A top gear ratio	6·021	5·175	4·840 **16**	4·684
No. gears	6	5	5	6

Model	GT380	GT550	GT750	RE5
Year	**1972–79**	**1972–77**	**1972–77**	**1974–77**
Fuel (l)	15	15	17	17
Engine oil (l)	1·3 **17**	1·3 **17**	1·8	2·5 + 1·7
Box oil (l)	1·4 **18**	1·5	2·2	1·6
Front fork/leg (cc)	210 **19**	235 **20**	235 **21**	150
Front tyre	3·00 × 19	3·25 × 19	3·25 × 19	3·25 × 19
Rear tyre	3·50 × 18	4·00 × 18	4·00 × 18	4·00 × 18
Front brake	180 drum **22**	2 × 200 drum **23**	2 × 200 drum **24**	dual 300 disc
Rear brake	180 drum	180 drum	180 drum	180 drum
Front suspension	teles	teles	teles	teles
Rear suspension	s/a	s/a	s/a	s/a
Ignition system	coil	coil	coil	points CDI
Wheelbase (in.)	53·4	55·3	57·8	59·1
Ground clear. (in.)	6·1	5·9	5·9	6·7
Width (in.)	33·5 **25**	33·5 **25**	34·0	34·3
Length (in.)	82·9 **26**	85·0 **27**	87·2	87·4
Dry weight (lb)	377	412 **28**	472 **29**	507

1 1975—6·9   **2** 1975—37   **3** 1975—53/7500   **4** 1975—70   **5** 1975—3·81   **6** 1975—5·35/6000
7 1975—8·50   **8** 1975—R, L—2·3, C—2·25; 1976—R, L—2·11, C—2·07   **9** 1975—2·85   **10** 1976—R, L—3·66, C—3·45
11 1974—15/36 (not USA)   **12** 1974—16/43, 1976 from engine 74191—15/40   **13** 1974—0·96 (not USA)
14 1974—0·96   **15** 1·76 from engine 73059—1·38 and 1·78   **16** 1974—4·324, 1976—4·291   **17** 1974—1·2
18 1974—1·5   **19** 1974—145   **20** 1974—160   **21** 1975—160   **22** 1973—275 disc   **23** 1973—295 disc   **24** 1973—dual 295 discs   **25** 1973—32·1   **26** 1973—82·3   **27** 1973—86·4   **28** 1973—441
29 1973—507

The following models were built for the Japanese home market and were only exported in limited numbers, if at all

Model	R50	MD	M50	80K
Year	**1961–62**	**1961–62**	**1969–77**	**1962**
No. cylinders	1	1	1	1
Bore (mm)		42	41	45
Stroke (mm)		38	37·8	50
Capacity (cc)	50	52·6	49·9	79·5
Compression ratio (to 1)		6·7	6·1	6·7
Power: bhp	7	4·5	1·8	6·5
@ rpm	11,000	8000	5000	6000

Specifications

	R50 1961–62	MD 1961–62	M50 1969–77	80K 1962
Torque (Kg-m)			0·3	
@ rpm			3000	
Valve type		piston		piston
No. gears	5	4	2	4
Tyre (in.)	2·25 × 17	2·25 × 17	2·00 × 17	2·50 × 17
Front suspension	leading link	leading link	trailing link	teles
Rear suspension	s/a	s/a	s/a	s/a
Wheelbase (in.)			42·9	
Width (in.)			24·8	
Length (in.)			66·9	
Dry weight (lb)			99	

Model	M80	K80	A90	K90
Year	1965	1967	1967–68	1967–69
No. cylinders	1	1	1	1
Bore (mm)	45	49	47	47
Stroke (mm)	50	42	50	50
Capacity (cc)	79·5	79·2	86·7	86·7
Compression ratio (to 1)	6·7	6·7	6·2	6·2
Power: bhp	6	6	8·4	8·4
@ rpm	6000	8500	7500	7500
Torque (Kg-m)		0·5	0·89	0·89
@ rpm		7500	5000	5000
No. gears	4	4	4	4
Tyre (in.)	2·25 × 17	2·50 × 17	2·50 × 17	2·50 × 17
Front suspension	leading link	teles	teles	teles
Rear suspension	s/a	s/a	s/a	s/a
Wheelbase (in.)	44·5	45·7	45·5	45·7
Width (in.)	27·2	26·2	26·8	26·8
Length (in.)	68·9	70·5	71·6	70·5
Dry weight (lb)	154	176	187	187

Model	AS90	AC90	K90G	F90
Year	1968	1968	1970–76	1970
No. cylinders	1	1	1	1
Bore (mm)	47	47	50	50
Stroke (mm)	50	50	45	45
Capacity (cc)	86·7	86·7	88·4	88·4
Compression ratio (to 1)	6·2	6·2	6·7	6·7
Power: bhp	8·4	8·4	7·5	7·5
@ rpm	7500	7500	6500	6500
Torque (Kg-m)	0·89	0·89	0·95	0·95
@ rpm	5000	5000	4500	4500
No. gears	4	4	4	3
Front tyre (in.)	2·50 × 18	2·50 × 18	2·50 × 17	2·75 × 14
Rear tyre (in.)	2·50 × 18	2·75 × 18	2·50 × 17	2·75 × 14

Suzuki Two-strokes

	AS90	AC90	K90G	F90
	1968	**1968**	**1970–76**	**1970**
Front suspension	teles	teles	teles	trailing link
Rear suspension	s/a	s/a	s/a	s/a
Wheelbase (in.)	46·8	46·8	46·6	46·7
Width (in.)	30·7	30·7	29·9	29·9
Length (in.)	72·4	72·4	71·5	71·5
Dry weight (lb)	191	198	189	180

Model	SH	S10	T90	T125
Year	**1961–62**	**1964–66**	**1969–70**	**1967–68**
No. cylinders	1	1	2	2
Bore (mm)	52	54	38	43
Stroke (mm)	58	54	39·6	43
Capacity (cc)	123	123·7	89·8	124·9
Compression ratio (to 1)	7·0	7·0	7·5	6·5
Power: bhp	8·0	10·5	10·5	15
@ rpm	6000	7000	9000	8500
Torque (Kg-m)			0·89	1·38
@ rpm			7000	7000
Valve type	piston			
No. gears	4	4	5	5
Front tyre (in.)	2·75 × 17	3·00 × 16	2·50 × 18	2·50 × 18
Rear tyre (in.)	2·75 × 17	3·00 × 16	2·50 × 18	2·75 × 18
Front suspension	teles	teles	teles	teles
Rear suspension	s/a	s/a	s/a	s/a
Wheelbase (in.)		49·6	47·2	48·6
Width (in.)		30·1	23·4	30·5
Length (in.)		74·8	71·6	77·8
Dry weight (lb)		257	216	279

Model	TC200	TC250	T21
Year	**1967**	**1967**	**1966–67**
No. cylinders	2	2	2
Bore (mm)	50	54	54
Stroke (mm)	50	54	54
Capacity (cc)	196·4	247	247
Compression ratio (to 1)	7·0	7·8	7·8
Power: bhp	21	30·5	30·5
@ rpm	7500	8000	8000
Torque (Kg-m)	2·09	2·82	2·82
@ rpm	7000	7000	7000
No. gears	5	6	6
Front tyre (in.)	2·75 × 18	3·00 × 18	2·75 × 18
Rear tyre (in.)	3·00 × 18	3·50 × 18	3·00 × 18
Front suspension	teles	teles	teles
Rear suspension	s/a	s/a	s/a
Wheelbase (in.)	49·4	50·6	50·6

	TC200 1967	TC250 1967	T21 1966–67
Width (in.)	30·5	30·1	30·1
Length (in.)	76·0	78·1	79·9
Dry weight (lb)	304	332	319

Names, numbers and letters

Suzuki have used over the years and continue to use a series of letter prefixes for their machines which are often confusing and seem to have little relation to one another. These letters are normally followed by the machine capacity but in their early days even that was denied to prospective customers and there was some difficulty for both dealer and owner.

They also gave various models names for a period but this practice died out in the seventies to leave the typing system. While the names were in use further problems arose in a few cases as a different name was used in the USA to the UK. Thus the 500 twin was the Titan in the USA but the Cobra in England as Titan was already being used by a major dealer for his own range of models modified in the cafe racer image.

From 1971 Suzuki began to use letter suffixes to denote a model type and approximate year. These continue for the off-road models and to some extent for others but there are exceptions and the letters are not used for all models.

Below are listed the various codes used by the firm.

Names

These are set out in two columns, one in alpha and capacity order and the other in the alphabetical order of the names so that they can be cross-referred either way.

A100	Charger	**Adventurer**	GT185
AC100	Wolf	**Apache**	TS400
AS100	Sierra	**Blazer**	TC100
B120	Student	**Cat**	TC120
F50	Cutlass	**Challenger**	TM125
GT185	Adventurer	**Champion**	TM250
GT250	Hustler	**Charger**	A100
GT380	Sebring	**Charger**	T500
GT550	Indy	**Cobra**	T500
GT750	Le Mans	**Cutlass**	F50
MT50	Trailhopper	**Cyclone**	TM400
RL250	Exacta	**Duster**	TS125

RV90	Rover	**Exacta**	RL250
RV125	Tracker	**Gaucho**	TS50
T20	Super Six	**Honcho**	TS100
T125	Stinger	**Hustler**	GT250
T200	Invader	**Hustler**	T250
T250	Hustler	**Indy**	GT550
T350	Rebel	**Invader**	T200
T500	Charger	**Le Mans**	GT750
T500	Cobra (UK)	**Prospector**	TC125
T500	Titan (USA)	**Rebel**	T350
TC100	Blazer	**Rover**	RV90
TC120	Trailcat	**Savage**	TS250
TC120	Cat	**Sebring**	GT380
TC125	Prospector	**Sierra**	AS100
TM125	Challenger	**Sierra**	TS185
TM250	Champion	**Stinger**	T125
TM400	Cyclone	**Student**	B120
TS50	Gaucho	**Super Six**	T20
TS100	Honcho	**Titan**	T500
TS125	Duster	**Tracker**	RV125
TS185	Sierra	**Trailcat**	TC120
TS250	Savage	**Trailhopper**	MT50
TS400	Apache	**Wolf**	AC100

Type and year code

1971	R	1976	A	1981	X
1972	J	1977	B	1982	Z
1973	K	1978	C	1983	D
1974	L	1979	N	1984	E
1975	M	1980	T		

Model letters

As found in this book:

A   horizontal engine, spine frame commuter

183

Suzuki Two-strokes

AC	sports A with raised exhaust	TR	production racing model
AP	model A with pedals for UK	TS	trail bike with single range gearbox
AS	sports A	U	step-thru model
B	fairly basic road single, spine frame	X	sports twin in USA (T20, T200, T250 models)
F, FR	step-thru model		
GA	A with engine protection bars		

and later:

GT	sports model, usually a twin, late single
K	utilitarian single, usually finished in black
KT	trail single, based on B model, spine frame
M	early singles, sports or touring
MT	small, off-road model, mini-bike
RA	works motocross 125, numbers after letters give year
RE	Wankel engine model
RH	works motocross 250, numbers after letters give year
RH	interim production motocross model
RL	trials model
RN	works motocross for 500 class, numbers as RH series
RN	interim production motocross model
RV	all terrain machine with fat tyres
RX	early Wankel engine model
S	early singles and twins, road models
T	early road twins
TC	trail single with dual range gearbox or early street scrambler twin
TM	early production motocross model

CL	scooter moped
CS	scooter, 2 or 4-stroke
DR	off-road 4-stroke
DS	trail 2-stroke
FS	2-stroke, step-thru, scooter moped
FZ	moped, step-thru
GN	4-stroke road single
GP	2-stroke road single
GS	4-stroke road single, twin or four
GS-T	custom version
GSX	sports version
JR	small off-road model
OR	custom moped, stands for 'on road'
PE	enduro model
RG	road racer model
RM	motocross model
RS	off-road 2-stroke
SB	commuter 2-stroke twin
SP	trail 4-stroke single
XN	turbo model
ZR	sports
ZR-L	custom

Model recognition

The identification of a machine is easy enough as the model number forms the prefix to the engine number stamped on the top of the left crankcase, the frame number stamped on the side of the steering head and is included on the machine plate rivetted to the headstock, these all being their normal locations.

Confirming the exact year is less easy and requires the use of engine and frame numbers and the help of the local importer. Due to the large quantities of machines built by Suzuki and the many countries in which they are sold, it is not practical to list all the engine and frame numbers, models and years without overstepping the bounds of these pages. Where the exact year is needed the local importer should be able to help on receipt of engine and frame numbers as the import documents will give the information required. If a machine has moved from one country to another, it may be necessary to trace it back to the point of original sale.

Colour information of the models in this book may also be established in a similar way. The variety offered and the many variables seen from year to year together with the complex striping used on modern machines would take an inordinate length to describe. In addition there are differences from country to country so that a machine offered in the choice of red or blue in one, may be green or white in another, and the position reversed or amalgamated for the following season.

The parts of the machine finished in colour are usually tank, side covers, mudguards, fork tops, headlamp shell, pivoted fork and rear chaincase but within that list for any one model and year some items may be black and others chrome-plated. The way to be sure as to the exact build is to consult the makers parts list. This gives the colour as a code in the part number, a chart of all the colours used in the list and notes on combinations where one part is finished in two colours.

To assist recognition of the various models, the notes below give some of their features which make them differ from similar machines. This information is to some extent a precis of the main text and should be used in conjunction with it and the other appendices.

All models have vertical or near vertical cylinder, telescopic front forks, pivoted fork rear suspension, wire spoke wheels and full width drum brakes unless otherwise stated.

Singles

A50	Horizontal cylinder, disc valve, low exhaust on right, 5 speeds, spine frame, chaincase
AC50	modified A50, raised exhaust on left, chainguard, forks gaitered or exposed springs
A50K	restricted A50 for UK
A50P	A50 with pedals for UK
AS50	as AC50
A70	as A50 except 4 speeds and capacity
A80	80 cc version of A70
A90	90 cc version of A70
AC90	sports A90, exhaust raised on left
AC90G	as AC90, detail changes
AS90	sports A90, exhaust low on right
AS90G	as AS90, detail changes
A100	100 cc version of A70
ACC100	sports A100, raised exhaust on left, new tank, seat, chainguard, mudguards, braced bars
ASS100	as ACC100 except exhaust low on right
A1ta	Welsh-built trials model with TC120 engine unit, special frame, tank, seat and REH forks
B100	basic single, 4 speeds, low exhaust on right, spine frame, chaincase
B100P	B100 with oil pump
B105P	trail model based on B100P with dual range, 3-speed gearbox
B120	later version of B100P, shrouded front forks, later called B120S
F50	step-thru, leading link forks, reed valve engine, enclosed fuel tank, separate rear mudguard, chaincase, one piece legshield
FR50	as F50 except rear mudguard part of frame
F70	70 cc version of F50
FR70	70 cc version of FR50
FR80	80 cc version of FR50
F90	90 cc version of step-thru, trailing link forks, 14 in. wheels
GA50	A50 with engine protection bars
GT100	disc valve engine, 5 speeds, tubular frame, disc front brakes
K10	piston port engine, 4 speeds, spine frame, downtube brace, low exhaust on right, valanced front mudguard, chaincase
K10P	K10 with oil pump
K11	as K10 except raised exhaust on right, narrow front mudguard, exposed fork springs
K11P	K11 with oil pump, gaitered front fork
K11T	trail version of K11 with new tank, mudguards, competition plates, universal tyres, raised and braced bars
K15	trail version of K11 with competition tyres, short seat, rear carrier, sprung front mudguard
K30	First version of K70
K50	utility version of A50 with reed valve and 4 speeds
KS50	K50 with raised exhaust
K80	as K10P, single seat
K90	90 cc version of K80 but horizontal engine and no downtube
K90G	as K90, revised engine
KT120	as B105P, fitted with rear carrier, raised exhaust on right
K125	disc valve engine with twin low exhausts, 4 speeds, spine frame, downtube brace, valanced front mudguard, chaincase; a utility model
M12	50 cc version of K11, no frame brace
M15	50 cc version of K10, no frame brace, leading link forks, Mark 2 version with telescopics
M15D	as M15 with electric start and 12 volt system
M30	step-thru, 3 speeds, automatic clutch, leading link forks, tank on frame supporting seat
M50	moped, 2 speeds, trailing link front forks
MT50	mini-bike with 3 speeds, spine frame, chunky 8 in. tyres, pressed steel wheels
M80	80 cc step-thru as M30
RH250	interim works replica motocross model
RL250	trials model, later built in UK
RL325	trials model
RN400	as RH250
RV50	all terrain model with spine frame, fat tyres, pressed steel wheels
RV75	75 cc version of RV50

Model recognition

185

Suzuki Two-strokes

RV90	90 cc version of RV50
RV90F	Farm bike version of RV90, big rear rack
RV125	125 cc version of RV50 with cradle frame
S10	early version of K125
TC90	trail model, dual range gearbox, exhaust high on left, rear carrier, disc valve
TC100	100 cc version of TC90, exhaust low on right
TC100F	Farm bike version of TC100, big rear rack
TC120	as KT120 in tubular spine type frame
TC125	piston ported engine, exhaust low and sloping up on right, dual range gearbox, L model with 21 in. front tyre
TC185	as TC125 except exhaust high on right, oil tank on left
TM75	motocross model, horizontal engine, exhaust low on right
TM100	motocross model, exhaust low on right
TM125	as TM100
TM250	as TM100
TM400	as TM100
TR50	road racing single
TR100	road racing single, disc front brake
TR125	as TR100
TS50	trail model with A50 engine, tubular spine frame, exhaust low and sloping up on right
TS75	as TS50
TS90	disc valve as TC90, no carrier, 5 speeds
TS100	as TC100 except 5 speeds, no carrier
TS125	as TC125 except 5 speeds, L model with 21 in. front tyre
TS185	piston ported, exhaust high on right, oil tank on left, J model with PEI, L model with 21 in. front tyre
TS250	as TS185
TS400	piston ported, exhaust low and sloping up on right, 5 speeds, PEI, L model with 21 in. front tyre
U50	step-thru as M30
U70	70 cc version of U50

Twins

S30	125, spine frame, front downtube, early models with one carburettor, later with two
S31	sports version of S30 with raised exhausts and twin carburettors
S32	150, as S30
T10	250, 4 speeds, spine frame, electric start, hydraulic rear brake
T20	250, 6 speeds, oil pump, tubular frame, left kickstart, cable rear brake
T21	high performance version of T20, exposed suspension springs
T125	as T200 at first, then changed to
T125	Stinger model, horizontal cylinders, 5 speeds, raised exhausts, tubular spine frame
T90	90 cc version of T125 Stinger
GT125	ram-air engine cooling, 5 speeds, alternator, disc front brake
GT125C	disc on left
GT125EC	cast alloy wheels
GT185	as GT125 except dynamo, electric starter, drum front brake, clutch lift different, from L model with single front disc
GT185EC	cast alloy wheels
T200	as T20 but smaller and 5 speeds
TC200	street scrambler version of T200
T250	as T20 except oil pump mounted on top of crankcase, first version with T21 engine
TC250	street scrambler version of T250 with T21 engine
GT250	ram-air cooling, disc front brake
GT250A	no ram-air, new barrels, 4 mains
T305	larger version of T20
T350	larger version of T250
T500	as T20 but 500 cc and 5 speeds
GT500	PEI, disc front brake, larger tank, no steering damper
TR250	racing version
TR500	racing version, air or water cooled

Triples

GT380	ram-air, 6 speeds, kickstart, remote points drive, drum front for J, disc for K and later
GT550	ram-air, 5 speeds, electric start, rev-counter crankshaft driven, from M model with chrome bores, double drum for J, disc for K and later
GT750	water cooled triple, double drum brake on J model, twin disc for K and later, L model with gear indicator and CV carburettors, M model with more power and no fork gaiters
TR750	road racing version
RE5	Wankel engine model—unique

Carburettor settings

The settings given below are for guidance only and represent those used for general market versions of each model. Specific countries often had their own set of figures which differed by varying amounts from those given. The model year is the total period it was in production and in some instances the settings may not apply to all years.

The fuel level was taken in a variety of ways but in most cases the point from which the figure is measured and the method will be clear to anyone familiar with the marque.

The figures given are taken from Suzuki material and thus should be correct. It is possible that the original data contained errors. For all these reasons it is best to check with the local importer as to the correct settings. If there is any doubt they should be confirmed with a carburation check. Always err to the rich side if in doubt as an oiled plug is less expensive than a holed piston.

Model	Year	Carb. bore	Main jet	Needle jet	Jet needle	Pilot jet	Pilot outlet	Starter jet	Air jet	Valve Seat	Bypass	Cut-away	Air screw	Fuel level
A50	1969–71	16	67·5	E–2	3G1–2	20	0·9	40		1·2		2·0	1½	22·5
A50	1972–76	16	72·5	E–2	3G1–3	25	0·9	40		1·2		2·0	1½	22·5
AC50	1970–71	16	70	E–2	3E3–3	20	0·9	40		1·2		2·0	1½	22·5
AC50	1972–76	16	75	E–2	3E3–3	17·5	0·9	40		1·2		2·0	1½	22·5
A50P	1975–77	16	72·5	E–2	3G1–3	25						2·0	1½	22·5
AS50	1969–70	16	70	E–2	3G1–2	20	0·9	40		1·2		2·0	2	22·5
M30	1963–67	15	120	E–0	15F1–3	15	0·9	30	0·7	1·2		1·0	1½	23
U50	1969	15	100	E–4	3L4–2	17·5	0·8	40	1·2	1·2		2·0	1¼	
U50	1970	15	65		3N3–3	17·5						2·0	1¼	23
F50	1970–71	14	102·5	E–0	3F3–3	17·5	0·9	40	2·0	1·2		2·5	1¼	23
F50	1972–73	14	107·5	D–8	3G9–4	17·5	0·9	40	2·0	1·2		2·5	1¼	24
FR50	1973–76	14	80	E–4	3L4–2	15	0·9	60		1·2		2·0	1¾	25
K50	1970	15	100		3J1–3	20						3·0	1¼	24·5
K50	1971	14	112·5		3E3–3	17·5						2·5	1¼	24·5
K50	1972–76	14	112·5	E–2	3F3–3	17·5	0·9	40	2·0	1·2		2·5	1¼	24
M15	1963–67	15	80	E–0	14F1–3	20			0·5			2·0	1¾	
MT50	1971–73	14	105	E–0	3G9–3	17·5	0·9	40	2·0	1·2		2·5	1½	24
RV50	1973–76	14	65	E–3	3E3–4	15		40				2·5	1½	24
TS50	1971–76	16	75	E–2	3E3–3	17·5	0·9	40		1·2		2·0	1½	22·5
A70	1970–71	16	120		3G1–3	30						2·5	2	22·5
A70	1972	15	120	E–2	3G1–3	30	0·9	30	0·5	1·2		2·5	2	22·5
U70	1970–71	15	90	E–0	3J1–3	25	0·9	40	0·5	1·2		2·5	2	22·5
F70	1972	15	82·5	E–2	3J1–2	17·5	0·8	40	0·5	1·2		2·5	1½	23
F70	1973	15	80	E–2	3J2–3	17·5	0·8	40	0·7	1·2		2·5	1¾	22·5
FR70	1973–76	15	77·5	E–2	3L4–3	15	0·8	50		1·2		2·0	1¼	25
FR70	1973–76	15	77·5	E–3	3H4–3	17·5	0·8	50		1·2		2·0	1¼	25
TM75	1974–76	16	77·5	E–3	3E3–3	22·5	0·9	40		1·0		2·0	1½	22·5
TS75	1974–77	16	77·5	E–3	3E3–3	22·5		40				2·0	1½	22·5
A80	1972–76	15	115	E–2	3J2–3	15	0·9	30	0·5	1·2		2·5	1¾	23
K10	1962–66	17	65	O–0	4J5–2	20	1·2	40	0·5/1·5	1·5		2·0	1½	
K11	1963–66	17	75	N–6	4J5–3	17·5	1·2	40	0·5/1·5	1·5		1·0	1¼	
RV90	1973–74	17	250	E–6	4J1–2	17·5	1·0	50	2·5	1·2		3·0	1¼	22·5
RV90	1975–76	17	250	E–6	4I2–3	17·5		50				3·0	1½	22·5
TC90	1970–71	19	180	E–1	5F12–3	17·5	0·6	80	0·9/0·5	2·0	1·4	2·5	1¼	25·1

Model	Year	Carb. bore	Main jet	Needle jet	Jet needle	Pilot jet	Pilot outlet	Starter jet	Air jet	Valve Seat	Bypass	Cut-away	Air screw	Fuel level
TC90	1972	19	150	E–1	5D3–3	17·5	0·6	80	0·9/0·5	2·0	1·4	2·0	$1\frac{1}{4}$	25·1
TS90	1970	19	170		5Q1–3	17·5						2·5	$1\frac{1}{2}$	25·1
TS90	1971	19	180	E–1	5F12–3	17·5	0·6	80	0·7/1·0	2·0	1·2	2·5	$1\frac{1}{2}$	25·1
TS90	1972	19	150	E–1	5D3–3	17·5	0·6	80	0·9/0·5	2·0	1·4	2·0	$1\frac{1}{4}$	25·1
A100	1967–80	20	75	E–0	5ES1–2	35	0·6	60		1·5	1·4	2·5	$1\frac{1}{2}$	25·1
TC100	1973–76	19	210	E–4	5D3–3	22·5	0·5	80	1·3		1·1	2·0	$1\frac{1}{2}$	25·1
TM100	1974–75	28	125	O–4	5DP7–4	30		90				2·0	$1\frac{1}{2}$	25
TS100	1973–77	19	200	E–4	5D3–3	22·5	0·5	80	1·3		1·1	2·0	$1\frac{1}{2}$	25·1
B100P	1966–70	20	95		4F11–2	25						2·0	$1\frac{1}{2}$	25·1
B100P	1966–70	20	95	N–2	4F9–4	25	1·4	40		1·5		2·0	$1\frac{1}{2}$	
B120	1970–74	20	95	N–2	4F11–2	25	1·4	30		1·5		2·0	$1\frac{1}{2}$	25·1
KT120	1967–69	20	100	O–0	4F10–3	25	1·4	30				2·5	1	25·1
TC120	1970	20	100		4D8–4	25						2·5	$1\frac{1}{2}$	25·1
TC120	1971–72	20	110	O–0	4D8–3	25	1·4	30		1·5		2·5	$1\frac{1}{2}$	25·1
K125	1970–71	21	130		4J6–2	20						3·0	$2\frac{1}{4}$	25·25
K125	1972–73	21	130	O–0	4J6–2	20	0·6	100	2·0	2·0	1·4	2·0	$2\frac{1}{2}$	25·25
K125	1974–76	21	140	O–0	4J6–2	25		100				2·0	$2\frac{1}{4}$	28
RV125	1973–77	22	110	P–2	4F10–4	20		80				3·0	$1\frac{1}{2}$	25·8
S10	1964		120	N–6	4J6–3	17·5		100				1·5		
TC125	1972	24	125	O–4	4DH5–2	25	0·7	80		2·0	1·4	3·0	$1\frac{1}{4}$	6·8
TC125	1973–76	24	90	O–0	4DH7–3	25	0·7	80		1·5	1·4	3·0	$1\frac{1}{4}$	6·8
TM125	1973–75	26	145	O–4	5DP7–3	30	0·6	80		2·8	1·4	2·0	$1\frac{1}{2}$	25·3
TS125	1971–73	24	125	O–4	4DH5–2	25	0·7	80		2·0	1·4	3·0	$1\frac{1}{4}$	6·8
TS125	1971–77	24	90	O–0	4DH7–3	25	0·7	80		1·5	1·4	3·0	$1\frac{1}{4}$	6·8
TC185	1974–76	24	130	O–4	5DP28–3	17·5		80				1·5	$1\frac{1}{2}$	17·3
TS185	1971–74	24	130	O–6	5DH4–2	25	0·7	80		2·0	1·4	2·5	$1\frac{1}{2}$	6·8
TS185	1975–77	24	125	O–4	5DH4–3	25		80				2·5	$1\frac{1}{2}$	17·3
RL250	1973–75	28	145	O–6	5CN6–3	30	0·7	80		2·5		2·0	$1\frac{1}{2}$	13·7
TM250	1972–73	32	260	Q–2	6FJ11–3	20	0·8	130		3·3	1·6	2·0	$1\frac{1}{2}$	9·1
TM250	1972–73	32	230	P–0	6DP1–2	40	0·8	130		3·3	1·6	1·5	1	9·1
TM250	1975	32	210	O–6	6DP1–2	35		130				1·5	$1\frac{1}{2}$	31·8
TS250	1970	28	115	P–2	5EP6–3	25	0·8	130		3·3	1·6	2·0	$1\frac{1}{4}$	28·3
TS250	1971–75	28	180	O–4	5CN3–2	25	0·9	80		2·5	1·2	2·5	$1\frac{3}{4}$	15·2
TS250	1976–77	28	140	O–9	5CN3–3	30						2·5	$1\frac{1}{2}$	14·6
TM400	1971–74	34	310	Q–8	6FJ6–3	35	0·8	40		3·3	1·6	2·0	$1\frac{1}{2}$	10·5
TM400	1971–74	34	250	P–3	6DH3–4	35	0·8	40		3·3	1·6	2·5	1	10·5
TM400	1975	34	280	Q–8	6FJ6–2	35		40				2·0	$1\frac{1}{2}$	23·4
TM400	1975	34	240	P–3	6DH3–3	40		40				2·5	1	23·4
TS400	1972–74	32	210	Q–6	6DP5–3	40	0·8	80		3·3	1·2	3·0	$1\frac{1}{4}$	31·75
TS400	1975–76	32	112·5	O–9	5F20–3	27·5		100				2·5	$1\frac{1}{4}$	27·3
T125	1969–73	18	72·5		4F13–4	20	0·9	30	2·5	1·5		2·5	$1\frac{1}{2}$	19
GT125	1974	18	70	N–8	4F19–3	25	1·0	50		1·3		2·5	$1\frac{1}{2}$	19·9
GT125	1980	19	77·5	P–4	4J31–4	17·5	1·0	50	0·7	1·3		2·5	2	19·9
GT185	1973–75	20	72·5	N–4	4D17–3	20		40				2·0	1	19·9
GT185	1976–79	20	72·5	N–5	4D17–3	20	1·2	40		1·2		1·5	1	19·9
T200	1967–70	22	140		4DG6–3	25						2·5	$1\frac{1}{2}$	25·1

Model	Year	Carb. bore	Main jet	Needle jet	Jet needle	Pilot jet	Pilot outlet	Starter jet	Air jet	Valve Seat	Bypass	Cut-away	Air screw	Fuel level
T10	1963–67	20	70	N–6	24A–4	30	0·6		1·3	2·5	1·4	2·5	$1\frac{1}{2}$	25
T20	1966–68	24	95	N–6	4DH5–3	35		50		2·0		2·5	$1\frac{3}{4}$	25
T250	1969	24	87·5	N–6	4DH5–3	30	0·6	50	0·5	2·0	1·4	2·5	$1\frac{1}{2}$	25·7
T250	1970	26	110		5CN3–3	25						2·5	$1\frac{1}{2}$	
T250	1971–72	26	110	O–2	5CN3–2	25	0·6	80		2·5	1·2	2·5	$1\frac{1}{2}$	13·7
GT250	1973–74	26	110	O–2	5CN3–2	25	0·6	80		2·5	1·2	2·5	$1\frac{1}{2}$	13·7
GT250	1975	26	112·5	O–2	5CN3–3	25		80				2·5	$1\frac{1}{2}$	17·3
GT250	1976–78	28	92·5	O–2	5CN3–3	30		100				2·5	$1\frac{1}{2}$	13·6
T305	1968–69	32	170		5DP2–3	30						2·5	$1\frac{1}{2}$	27·25
T350	1969	32	170	Q–0	5DP2–3	30	0·6	60		2·5	1·4	2·5	$1\frac{1}{2}$	27·5
T350	1969	32	112·5		5DP2–2	30						2·5	$1\frac{1}{2}$	27·25
T350	1970	32	112·5		5D13–4	35						2·5	$1\frac{1}{2}$	27·25
T350	1971–73	32	112·5	P–6	5DL13–4	35	0·6	40		2·5	1·4	2·5	$1\frac{1}{2}$	27·25
T500	1967–68	34	410		5DP2–2	25						2·5	$1\frac{1}{2}$	30·3
T500	1969–70	32	150	P–4	5FP8–3	30	0·6	70		2·5	1·4	2·5	$1\frac{1}{4}$	27·25
T500	1971–72	32	150	P–5 P–4	5FP8–3	30	0·6	70		2·5	1·4	2·5	$1\frac{1}{4}$	27·25
T500	1975	32	97·5	P–4	5FP17–3	30		70				2·5	$1\frac{1}{2}$	27·3
GT500	1976–77	32	97·5		5FP17–3	30						2·5		27·3
GT380	1972–73	24	80	O–4	4DH7–2	22·5	0·8	60		2·0	1·4	3·0	$1\frac{1}{4}$	24·25
GT380	1975	24	80	O–2	4DH7–2	25		80				3·0	$1\frac{1}{4}$	25·8
GT550	1972–73	28	95, C–92·5	O–5	5DH21–3	27·5	0·5	60		2·0	1·4	2·5	$1\frac{1}{4}$	24·25
GT550	1972–73	28	87·5, C–85	O–2	5C4–3	25	0·5	60		2·0	1·4	2·0	$1\frac{1}{4}$	24·25
GT550	1975	28	100	O–8	5DH21–4	25		110				2·5	$1\frac{3}{4}$	25·8
GT750	1972–73	32	102·5, C–100	P–4, C–P–3	5F16–3	30	0·6	50		2·5	1·4	2·5	$1\frac{1}{2}$	27·25
GT750	1975	40	110, C–107·5	Z–0	4DN18–4	45	0·7	110		2·3			$\frac{3}{4}$	27·6
					choke			Air bleed	Pilot air jet					
RE5	1974–77	18	87·5		15	45		80	145	3·0				43·3
		32	180		27 × 8	70		80	140					

Model chart

Model	1962	63	64	65	66	67	68	69	70	71	72	73	74	75	76	77	78	79
M15																		
M12																		
M30																		
U50																		
F50																		
FR50																		
A50																		
AS50																		
AC50																		
A50P																		
A50K																		
KS50																		
K50																		
M50																		
MT50																		
RV50																		
TS50																		
U70																		
F70																		
FR70																		
K30																		
A70																		
RV75																		
TM75																		
TS75																		
TS75							P	P										
K10/K10P						P	P	P										
						P	P											
K11/K11P																		
K11T																		
K15																		
M80																		
K80																		
A80																		
FR80																		
A90																		
F90																		
K90																		
TC90																		
TS90																		
RV90																		
A100																		

Suzuki Two-strokes